10 Useful Resources 173

Index 187

1 The Role of a Leader

*Leadership means different things
to different people. Whether you
are leading a small project team,
a sports team or a multi-national
organization, the principles of
leadership are the same. In this first
chapter we explore what leadership is
and how it can positively impact an
organization's performance.*

Introduction

Attend a training course or seminar on leadership, and it's quite likely that during one of the early sessions you'll be asked to take part in an exercise that involves listing a number of well-known, successful leaders. This exercise typically elicits responses such as Mahatma Gandhi; Franklin D Roosevelt; or even England's Queen Elizabeth I. From the business world, names typically cited include Steve Jobs (Apple CEO); Henry Ford (founder of the Ford motor Company) and Richard Branson (founder of the Virgin brand). All great leaders... there's no doubt.

Individuals are then typically asked to draw out similarities in leadership styles between each of their examples in the hope that these will provide clues to possible leadership characteristics and styles that might correlate to success.

It's a fun exercise. However, having experienced this exercise very many times, I think that probably the only significant message to be drawn from it is that there isn't just one ideal leadership style – in reality there are very many different styles of leadership that can, in their own way, be highly effective.

It's important to be yourself

This should be seen as a very liberating conclusion. Being an excellent leader isn't about trying to emulate someone else's style. It's certainly not about trying to adopt a style of leadership that's out of step with your style and personality. We want to encourage you to spend time learning about yourself and your strengths and then to develop a style of leadership that works for you.

Don't forget

Being an excellent leader is about being yourself, not trying to emulate other excellent leaders.

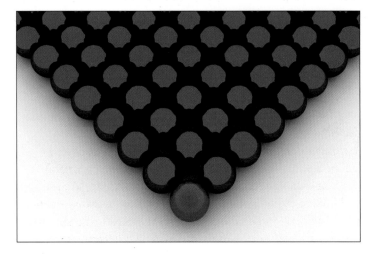

As as you read this book, don't just take the ideas and concepts that are described at face value – don't slavishly follow the techniques as they're written. Instead, stop and consider how they can specifically work for you. Ask yourself:

- Are these techniques or ideas ones I should be practicing?

- How well do they fit with my personal values? (this is something we'll look at in the next chapter)

- How do these ideas fit with my personality traits? (again, something we'll cover in the next chapter)

- If it isn't something I can imagine adopting, how can I manage using alternative solutions?

Comfort zone

Whilst encouraging you to question the ideas in this book in order to understand how they'll work for you, don't use this as an excuse not to try things out; to continue with your current style or to convince yourself that your methods are very similar anyway.

You may be tempted to stick within your comfort zone and either avoid trying something different or try it briefly and then return to your old ways. Some of the techniques may prove very easy to put in place. Expect that more fundamental changes – especially to deep-seated behaviors – may take longer to embed and, as a result, initially feel very awkward to perform.

Learning to drive

If you're a car driver and can remember back to your early attempts at learning to drive, you may recall that some of the techniques and skills you were asked to try felt very unnatural at first. You may have even wondered whether you could ever become an accomplished driver. After just a few months' practice, however, you will have gained sufficient experience to be able to drive competently without needing to think about your actions.

Hot tip

Be prepared to experiment with new techniques and behaviors. You may not get things right first time but be prepared to persevere.

6

Leaders Are Critical

You must have heard it. Employees saying how they feel they would be so much better off without their bosses. 'What value do they add to the working process?' 'Why do they need their boss?' 'Working life would be so much easier if they were just allowed to get on with their job... after all, their boss doesn't even know what they do half the time.'

Alarm bells

These complaints may or may not be valid but they're certainly not an indication that leadership isn't needed. They are more likely to be indications of other possible problems relating to a manager's style of leadership and this needs investigating.

In favour of leadership

So let's look at some of the key reasons why having leadership is so important. Excellent leaders will:

- Provide direction and focus at an individual and team level

- Ensure the climate in which people work is positive

- Ensure that the right resources are available and applied to the most appropriate activities

- Inspire people so they remain motivated and committed

- Recognise and develop people

- Ensure decisions are made effectively so things happen

Beware

If people complain that leaders in the organization are not adding value, it probably means that there is something wrong with the way they're applying themselves as leaders.

Direction and focus

Providing direction and focus is a critical element of Leadership. However well-intentioned people are, without someone to decide and communicate the direction in which the team is expected to be going in, there is a strong likelihood that people will channel their energies in less than productive ways.

Without leadership individuals can find themselves overlapping their activities with others' and duplicating effort or, alternatively, inadvertently leaving gaps in processes.

Some individuals may choose their own direction based on personal motivations. At worst, a whole team's activities could veer off in a wrong direction.

Climate

Put simply, climate can be described as 'how it feels to work around here.' The leader plays a key role in ensuring the climate people work in is positive. A positive climate is fundamental to delivering peak performance.

There are many elements that impact the climate within which people work, each of which can and should be measured. We'll look at these in more detail later in this chapter.

Hot tip

As an effective leader, focus your attention on trying to ensure the climate in the organization is positive.

11

Decision-making

This is a critical function of an effective leader. Poor or slow decision making can lead to:

- A lack of confidence from those awaiting a decision

- The wrong decision being made leading to exposure to risk and potential financial or reputational loss

- Missed opportunities in the intervening time

- People misdirected to work on inappropriate activities

All of these are very likely to have a significant impact on the performance of those working under a leader.

Why We All Need Leaders

Anyone who's experienced a truly excellent leader will understand what a positive and motivating experience it can be. Rather than feeling that the leader is a drag on their ability to get things done, they see their leader as someone who inspires and brings out the very best performance from them. If the leader has developed the right climate, they may not even necessarily need to be very conspicuous in their role as leader.

Positive benefits

Here are just a few of the ways in which people can benefit from working for an excellent leader. They will:

- Understand their role and how the work they do contributes towards the overall goals

- Feel a sense of worth about their role

- Have been encouraged to take their own personal development seriously

- Be confident they can ask questions, make suggestions and provide feedback, knowing they will be listened to

- Feel they can take (calculated, managed and appropriate) risks and feel they're supported

- Know they are trusted and empowered to act

- Feel an appropriate level of stretch and challenge in the things they do

Don't forget

Trust works both ways. As a leader, you want employees to trust you but you also need to have trust in your team.

Taking a Step Back

Leading from the front

It is often stated that leaders should be prepared to lead from the front. But this commonly used expression 'leading from the front' can be misleading and needs some clarification.

Typically this expression conjures up a war-torn battle scene with a commander heroically leading troops into battle, deep into enemy territory. This, of course, is some way off the reality of most modern leadership situations.

This type of leadership suggests a very hands-on or directive style with the leader getting stuck in with the delivery along with the rest of the team. This is generally not what a leader is expected to do unless they truly need to be a 'player-manager'.

Too much direct involvement can take a leader away from the things he or she should be doing. Followers are more likely to divert their energies towards trying to emulate their leader rather than be inspired to develop themselves and their roles. It can also discourage any sense of responsibility or empowerment.

The leader's perspective

As a leader you may need to pull yourself back from interfering with the delivery (unless this truly is a part of your role) and, instead, focus on getting the very most from those responsible and experienced at delivering. This is not about being elitist but it is ultimately about giving people clarity of direction and the support to help develop themselves and take responsibility.

Hot tip

The next time you are about to get involved in the detail, make a conscious effort to step back and focus on the big picture.

13

Leading vs. Managing

There is a big difference between leading and managing – it's worth clarifying the difference.

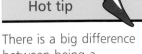

Hot tip

There is a big difference between being a manager and being a leader. Ensure you are clear of the difference.

Being a manager

Many people have 'manager' in their job title but this doesn't necessarily mean that they are a leader of people. It's possible to be a manager of a function or process, (for example, an Accounts Manager) without having to lead people. If you do have people reporting to you, there are two key functions to your role:

● Managing people

● Leading people

In many ways these two activities need to be interrelated but the function of managing people, if separated out from leading people, can be seen merely as managing a set of processes just like any other business process. Activities will include:

● Directing and prioritizing work and delegating responsibilities

● Ensuring people have the necessary skills to do their work effectively

● Setting goals and standards and monitoring performance especially through appraisals

● Managing individuals' attendance; sickness; holidays; payroll etc

Cold and directive

It's possible (although far from ideal) to perform these activities as management activities without performing as a leader. Sadly, this is the case for many managers who seem to be able to manage people in a cold and process-orientated way and, as a result, don't maximize the full potential of their people.

Dealing with attendance, sickness, and holidays etc are, of course, still management functions that you may have to perform as part of your role but these should not be confused with leadership.

Blending the two

Being an effective leader is about applying leadership activities to many of the managerial functions. For example, delegating work – or rather, responsibilities – can be considered as an opportunity to empower and grow an individual.

Developing others

Determining training needs can and should be so much more than just identifying and resolving knowledge and skills gaps to enable an individual to do their job. Development from a leadership perspective means helping an individual to recognize their own development needs; giving them the confidence to perform their role excellently. It also means dedicating time to help guide them towards achieving their career aspirations.

By fostering the right environment, individuals can be encouraged to see every experience as developmental – as opportunities to assess themselves in different situations and learn from them.

Setting goals

As a leader, setting goals takes on a very different meaning. Instead of setting goals in a directive, boss-centred manner, leaders approach goal-setting as an opportunity to understand an individual and their motives. Goal setting becomes a joint activity where the individual is involved and empowered to play an active role in determining what needs to be achieved. What is more, they should have sufficient clarity about their role and overall organizational purpose to do so confidently.

15

Hot tip

Goal setting is best when it comes from the individual who, as a result, is likely to be more motivated to meet their own goals than those imposed by you.

Effects of Good Leadership

The impact of providing excellent leadership is not just a handful of vague 'warm and fluffy' feelings. The net outcomes should be very tangible and, most importantly, measurable. A direct link can be made between leadership behaviors and practices and the hard bottom-line performance of the organization.

Don't forget

Truly excellent leadership results in tangible and measurable performance improvements.

16

Leadership and processes

As we have already suggested, leadership behaviors have a direct impact on an organizational climate. You will see from the above diagram that a leaders' behaviors also have an impact on the organizational processes involved – for example, how people communicate with one another; how people make decisions; how people know what do etc.

Individuals' motivations

Of course, individual team members will have their own personal motivations and these, in turn, will impact overall performance. It is up to the leader to understand individuals' motivations and so work with each member of the team to ensure they remain energized and personally motivated whilst at the same time contributing positively towards the organizational goals.

Beware

However excellent the leadership is, and however perfect the processes are, the human factor of individuals' own motivations should not be underestimated.

Clarity of Roles

Delivering consistently high performance within an organization requires more than just recruiting or retaining effective and motivated people. It is also essential that each individual is clear about his or her role and that they understand:

- How their role contributes towards the delivery of the organization's goals

- How their role needs to interact and communicate with others' roles in the organization

- How their role impacts others' roles i.e. who is dependent upon the outputs of their work

- What they need from others in order to perform their role (including support from their leader)

Part of this clarity comes from having well-defined structures and job definitions, part comes from how the leader communicates with individuals and delegates responsibilities.

Gaps and overlaps

Without sufficient clarity, there is a real danger that some roles will, to some degree, overlap. This can result in duplication of effort and wasted resource.

From a motivational point of view, individuals are likely to feel they've wasted their time and so may think twice about putting in so much effort in future. It can also lead to friction between the affected individuals who may feel their work or responsibilities are being high-jacked by the other.

Just as bad – especially from a customer's point of view – is for any lack of clarity in roles to result in gaps between roles where processes or responsibilities are not picked up by someone or only get picked up by chance.

Hot tip

Ask individuals to review their own roles and ask them whether they experience any duplication of effort due to overlapping roles.

Creating a Positive Climate

You'll note from the diagram on page 16 that the organizational climate combined with the processes adopted are the most significant factors affecting performance in any organization and both of these are inextricably linked to a leader's behaviors. We'll explore leadership behaviors in detail in the next chapter. When we refer to organizational climate we are talking about factors such as:

- How clear people are about their roles and their contribution to the overall mission

- How empowered and trusted people feel in order to be able to work effectively within the scope of their roles

- How well people are recognized for their contribution towards achieving the organizational goals

- How defined and how flexible processes and structures are to support the work people do

- How people are developed to meet the needs of the organization as well as individuals' personal aspirations

In organizations where people are clear about their roles; empowered to work; recognized for their contribution and supported and developed, the resultant climate will be positive and, as a result, organizational output maximized.

Getting it right

All this sounds quite logical and straightforward. Yet, so often, managers don't get around to doing these things. This can be due to an over-enthusiasm to get things done; because they don't recognize the need to do these things or because they just don't know how to.

Hot tip

Excellent leaders look out for opportunities to recognise and acknowledge high performance by their people.

Translating the vision

Some leaders are described by others (or sometimes by themselves!) as visionaries – an important leadership attribute – but unless they're able to translate and communicate their ideas to those that need to deliver the vision, their visions will be wasted.

Similarly, once leaders have communicated the vision, they must be able to motivate, empower and energise people so that they work with the leader towards achieving that vision.

Beware

Being a visionary is more than just having inspirational ideas. They also need to be able to communicate these so that others can help turn them into reality.

Confidence in others

One of the most important lessons to learn as a leader is to have confidence in those that work for and with you. Being a leader doesn't mean having all the answers. The higher up you are in an organization the less you are likely to need to know about the day-to-day operational detail and the more you need to trust others to focus on this and instead keep you appraised of progress.

Being a leader does not, as is often described, need to be a lonely role. Although final decisions and the vision may be signed off by the leader, they're likely to benefit from consultation with others who can bring to the table a number of different perspectives. This is something we'll explore in Chapter 4.

Developing yourself and others

There is a direct correlation between those who take personal development seriously – of themselves and others – and top performance. People who are encouraged to take responsibility for their own development are far more likely to be engaged, motivated and energized in all that they do. These are all factors that contribute towards creating a positive climate.

Measuring The Impact

Measuring climate

The fact that the impacts of leadership behaviors can be traced right through to bottom-line performance means that it is possible – and advisable – to put in place a range of hard and soft measures to track the effectiveness of the organization and, in particular, the impact of leadership at various levels.

Measures can be used to keep a regular check on the climate of a whole organization, specific departments, or individual teams. By regularly monitoring, every 6 months or even annually, you can maintain a check on critical elements relating to the organizational climate – in particular, leadership behaviors – and so take action to bring about changes where necessary.

Here are just a few examples of possible measures:

- Employee surveys

- Customer satisfaction surveys

- Customer correspondence (praise and complaints)

- 360 degree feedback surveys on leadership

- Appraisal ratings and related verbatim comments

- Employee focus groups

- Prevalence of employee grievances

Hot tip

Using external help to assist with measuring climate can be very beneficial. Not only are they experts but they can also bring with them an independent perspective.

Getting help

You may be able set in place some measures without calling on specialist help but it can prove beneficial to get help from an external organization that can bring experience, independence and the opportunity to benchmark with other organizations.

This is especially the case when looking to design a robust 360 degree survey. This ideally requires the collection and interpretation of anonymous responses from employees, bosses and potentially customers on leaders' behaviors.

Making sense of the information

The effects of leadership, when measured across an organization can be very noticeable. Where there are layers of leadership in an organization, the positive climate encouraged and fostered by one leader can be either positively reinforced by the leader working immediately below them or, conversely, it can be negatively impacted or diluted depending on the quality of the leader at the next level down.

This is shown in the following diagram:

Beware

Don't assume, just because you have set in place a positive climate, that this will automatically flow through the whole organization.

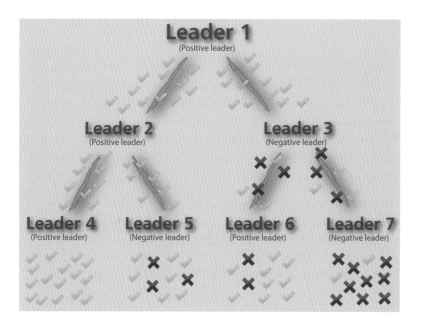

In this scenario, Leader 1 has, through effective leadership behaviors, created a positive climate (represented by the green check symbols). Leader 2, who is working under this positive climate has also created a positive climate, so reinforcing the overall positive climate.

Leader 3, on the other hand, through poor leadership behaviors, has reduced the overall positive climate (the negative impact is represented by the red crosses.

In the third layer, the individual leadership styles have, again either reinforced or weakened the overall leadership climate leading to very different climates, all within the same organization.

Leadership at All Levels

It's easy to fall into the trap of thinking that examples of excellent leadership are only to be found at the very top of large multi-national organizations or governments. These are the examples we hear about in the media but excellent leadership happens at all levels of an organization. Here are just a couple of real examples:

Leading despite the overall culture

This first example highlights the way in which a leader can directly impact the culture of the people working under them. The overall performance of the organization – a financial services company – was suffering due to poor overall leadership, a lack of direction and a heavily directive, almost dictatorial style of leadership being imposed from the very top of the organization.

Having been asked to conduct a climate survey across the business I was not surprised to find that the overall climate of the organization scored poorly across most indicators. I did notice, however, that the results of one particular department, consisting of approximately 20% of the business, bucked the overall trend. Some indicators were similar but many others appeared far more positive, as if the results were from a different organization.

Micro climate

Investigating further it became clear the leader of this department, a middle manager we'll call Julie, was working hard to create a very different climate under which the people in her department could continue to operate effectively, despite the overall negative leadership climate which she was having to contend with.

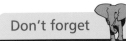

Don't forget

You can be a leader whatever your position in an organization if you are in a position to influence others.

Julie was having to work especially hard, acting as a buffer or shield so that her teams were exposed as little as possible to the overall negative organizational climate.

Julie was effectively creating her own positive micro-climate – something that took all her energy to achieve but meant that those in Julie's department could still continue to deliver top performance despite the overall business performance.

Leading from the bottom

This second inspiring example demonstrates that it is possible to lead whatever your level in an organization. It involved a junior administrator, Adam, who worked within a customer services team within a major IT software company.

Adam's work was relatively routine and, it has to be said, not very exciting or demanding. As part of a general drive for improvement the company bosses put out a request for all staff to suggest ways in which the organization could be more customer focussed. Predictably, suggestions mainly came from senior management whilst more junior staff were either apathetic about the scheme or reluctant to make suggestions, believing their ideas would be ignored anyway.

Adam, on the other hand, saw this as an opportunity to bring into being an idea he had been considering for some time. He preferred to take personal responsibility for making his idea happen and so, having gained permission from his bosses, called a meeting of his fellow team-mates.

Having won them over, he arranged brainstorming meetings to refine the precise details for a customer campaign which would involve regular personalized contact with the whole client base.

The rest of his colleagues bought into his proposed scheme based on Adam's sheer enthusiasm and belief in his idea. The end result was an improvement in the company's 'mystery shopper' scores by a factor of 180% over a 12 month period.

Hot tip

Allow people to take responsibility for working things through themselves and they may just surprise you with their willingness to take the lead.

23

Variety is The Spice...

Leadership models can be useful in helping to understand the underlying processes involved. There are, however, limitations to many models or defined processes. Firstly, they cannot take into account your own style and personality – they have to describe processes that will work for the majority of people and for the majority of situations. Secondly, unless flexibility is specifically built in, they often only provide a single approach to a situation.

So many variables

In reality, very rarely will there be only one possible approach to a situation. If there were, the role of a leader would be straightforward. In the real world there are normally very many variables that will all impact your choice of approach:

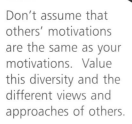

24

- Your personality, motivations and skill-base

- The individual's personality, motivations and skills

- The nature of the issue being addressed

- Previous interactions you've had with the individual

- The specific mood of the individual (and of you)

- A whole range of external circumstances that can each have an impact on the issue

If you're familiar with the concept of 'chaos theory' you will understand and appreciate that there are an infinite number of permutations of the above factors, all of which can subtly affect the way just one leadership interaction could unfurl.

Flexibility is the key

Given so many possible ways in which a scenario could play out, it's essential that you remain flexible to be able to respond to situations as they develop. You certainly need to become acutely aware of your own capabilities, motivations and personality profile. These are at least things which you can have some control over.

The impact of your personality

In the next chapter we're going to explore various aspects of personality in order to help you understand how each element can significantly affect the way you are likely to approach different leadership challenges and their subsequent outcomes.

Keep an open mind

At this stage, it is enough to say that you should keep an open mind to a wide range of different approaches especially those you have not tried before.

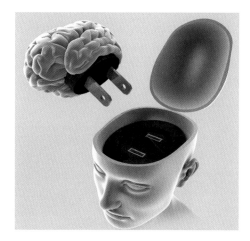

Even where you have previously experimented with new approaches and techniques, try to keep an open mind as you read through the ideas described in this book. Too often, individuals will try a new idea once and then abandon it – either because it didn't work first time or because they just haven't given it time to bed in and become a natural way of acting.

Your options

Even if a leadership technique or behavior is not one that comes naturally, you still have a number of options:

- Persevere to develop the behavior over time

- Understand that this is not your strength and use alternative approaches

- Manage the problem by using someone else who you recognize as having this strength

Don't forget

If you discover a particular leadership behavior is difficult for you to deliver, you can always find someone else to support you who is strong in that area.

Learning From Your Past

Studying examples of excellent leadership from management texts, magazines and online articles can be enlightening. It is important to remember, however, that these examples are based on other leaders' experiences and personal styles.

Past bosses

It can also be a worthwhile exercise to examine examples from your own past. During your working life – and possibly also from outside of work – you may have experienced examples of excellent leadership in action.

Perhaps you can recall individuals who have stood out for you as exceptional leaders. These examples can be of particular value if they were your bosses. Think back to what made these leaders stand out as being so exceptional to you and the impact they had on your working environment. Ask yourself:

Hot tip

Look up one of your old bosses whose leadership style you respected. Invite them for a social and find out more about their views on leadership.

26

- In what ways was the climate of the organization positively affected by this leader's behaviors and actions?

- What did the climate feel like that resulted from this leader's behaviors?

- How did I and others around me respond to their leadership style

- What learning can I take from these examples that I could apply to my own personal leadership behaviors and style?

Remember the detail

It will be far more useful to you if you can remember some of the detail within your examples. Try to recall specific instances – perhaps key defining moments – that illustrate the positive behaviors of your exemplar boss. If you can, take yourself back to these defining moments and re-enact them in your mind in order to bring out the precise detail.

Speak to them

Very few people get the opportunity to meet and pick the brains of any of the well-known global leaders. You may have more luck interviewing or just chatting with one of your old bosses or respected colleagues about their leadership style. Find an opportunity to ask them a few questions about their attitudes to leadership or some of the techniques they have employed.

Whilst your discussion may be relatively informal, try to ensure your questions are focussed and specific. If your questions are too broad, such as: "What do you think makes a good leader" they may struggle to give you useful responses. Give them space to think and perhaps even email you their thoughts at a later date.

Learning from bad examples

Sadly, many of us are just as likely to have experienced leaders who have negatively impacted the work environment and the performance of those that have worked for them.

These can still help you understand and adapt your own style, if only by highlighting the negative impacts of certain leadership behaviors and styles therefore providing you with pointers about how you don't want to behave or be perceived!

Don't copy

As we warned at the beginning of this chapter, it is important that you draw lessons from all these rich, real-life examples rather than try to emulate or copy them directly. In the next chapter we will be examining leadership behaviors in more detail to help you to understand your own behavioral strengths.

Beware

You need to develop a leadership style that's right for you. Don't copy. Just learn from what you see and hear – above all, be true to yourself.

Other Performance Factors

There's no doubt that the single most important element affecting an organization's performance is the application of leadership behaviors. However, as we briefly touched upon on Page 16, there are other factors that affect performance and these are most likely also in the leader's control.

Structures

However competent and motivated people are, the structures within which individuals and teams are expected to work can have a significant impact on overall performance.

Take a look at the structures within your organization. Do they:

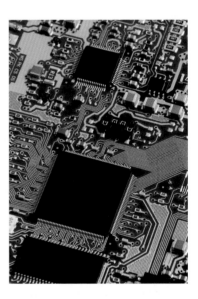

- Support processes such that they enable rather than hinder their execution?

- Support and enable effective and timely decision-making?

- Ensure the least possible duplication of effort?

- Minimise wastage of time and resources?

- Provide the most effective reporting lines?

- Ensure that effective communication can take place between individuals and teams?

Hot tip

Take a step back from the organization from time to time to review whether the structure is still the most appropriate – especially after times of significant change.

Legacy structures may have evolved over time as new functions and processes have been added. These evolutionary changes in structures can gradually lead to inefficient working.

As a leader, from your strategic standpoint, you can ensure these issues are regularly considered and evaluated. If you're not involved in the day-to-day detail of the organization you'll probably need to involve others to evaluate the effectiveness of the current structures and, where necessary, to implement any changes.

Reporting structures

Much has been written on the merits or otherwise of flat reporting structures within organizations. Certainly there has been a general movement more recently away from hierarchical or pyramid structures towards flatter or horizontal structures

Steeply pyramidal reporting structures such as the one shown above mean fewer direct reports to manage but can also result in many leadership layers with deeper chains of communication. Flatter structures, stripped of management layers and associated costs, may be more efficient but care needs to be taken to ensure effective communication happens across the business.

Internal communication

Whilst this is just one of many processes that impact performance, it is probably the most critical. Internal communication is not just about how messages are delivered *down* an organization – this is probably quite easy to implement. The most important and often neglected channels of internal communication are those *between* teams and individuals.

Equally, attention needs to be given to *upward* communication channels to ensure that comments, ideas and feedback can find their way up to those that need to hear.

Effective leaders spend less of their time telling and more time listening to those who are on the ground with the relevant experience and exposure to what is happening.

Don't forget

Internal communication is one of the most important processes. Without it, it's impossible for an organization to function coherently.

Summary

- It's important to develop a leadership style that works for you, your personality and your values rather than trying to be someone else

- Having said that, be prepared to give things a go – try new techniques that may push you out of your 'comfort zone'

- Become known for being a leader that inspires others and adds value rather than one who gets in the way of things getting done

- An important role of a leader is to provide a sense of direction to ensure everyone is aligned to the overall mission and pulling in the same direction

- Effective decision-making should be done with appropriate levels of consultation with those that can contribute. This is not the same as decision-making by committee

- People thrive in organizations where there is effective leadership. They will feel encouraged; involved; supported and developed

- Excellent leadership is likely to seriously and positively affect your organization. There are many measurable elements of leadership that can be tracked to very tangible bottom-line performance indicators

- Leadership behaviors directly impact the climate in which people operate. Climate – 'how it feels to work around here' – is one of the most significant factors affecting organizational performance

- You don't need to be working at the very top of an organization to demonstrate effective leadership, you can be a leader at any level including the most junior positions

- Don't fall into the trap of thinking there's only one way of tackling a leadership issue. Leadership models help you understand the underlying issues but be flexible enough to consider a range of options

- Organizational and team processes and structures play an important role in delivering excellent performance

2 Leadership Behaviors

Underpinning your leadership style is a complex range of factors relating to different aspects of your personality. This chapter explores these and helps you to understand why you are driven to behave the way you do. Try some of the suggested exercises to help you develop a better appreciation of your own personality profile.

Being True to Yourself

In Chapter 1 we stressed the importance of being yourself rather than merely trying to mirror others' leadership styles. This sounds easy to do but does make the assumption you fully understand and appreciate who you are in the first instance.

Nature vs. nurture

Much is written on the subject of personality and, in particular, the 'nature vs. nurture' debate. That is, are you the person you are because of 'nature', i.e. the genetic coding that you were born with or due to 'nurture', i.e. the way you were brought up and the experiences that you have encountered and learnt from throughout the various stages in your life?

The answer is, you are who you are due to a complex combination of both nature and nurture and you should be proud of the resultant personality you have become. This is one of the main reasons why, in terms of becoming a leader, you should try to be yourself rather than trying to be someone else.

Look back to your childhood

Because your personality has gradually developed based on a combination of genetics and the experiences in your life, you'll probably be able to recall important moments in your life – especially from your childhood – where some of your early thinking, values and motivations started to take shape.

Think back to your childhood now and try to recall the types of games and activities that gave you the greatest satisfaction. Now try to relate these to work and the activities you enjoy the most.

You may notice that there are similarities in some of your favorite activities and the work you enjoy. We'll explore this some more later in this chapter.

Hot tip

Looking back at some of the games you played as a child can help you understand why you enjoy doing the things you do in your work life today.

Be genuine

One of the critical elements of being an excellent leader is trust. You need to be able to have trust in those who work for you and with you. Most essentially, others must have trust in you – it cannot be a one way thing.

Trust is a fragile thing that can only be built over time but with the possibility of being lost in an instant following, perhaps, just one careless comment or act. The people who interact with you have learnt who you are and will be acutely aware of any changes in your behaviors and actions.

If you aren't genuine – attempting to be someone who you are not – they will be quick to see through your facade or act and will be immediately on guard.

Tell them what you're doing

If you have an open enough relationship with those who you work with, you should be able to make them aware that you are working on aspects of your leadership. Ask them for help by:

- Giving you feedback on any positive changes they notice

- Letting you know if any of the changes don't appear genuine

- Letting you know of changes they would like to see happen

- Hopefully supporting you and encouraging you – after all, these changes should ultimately benefit them!

Beware

You cannot expect others to trust you if you are not prepared to demonstrate a level of trust for them – it works two ways.

Behind Excellent Leaders

Behind every excellent leader... well, behind every one of us, in fact, is a highly complex and constantly changing mix of personality elements that make up 'you'. These include aspects such as:

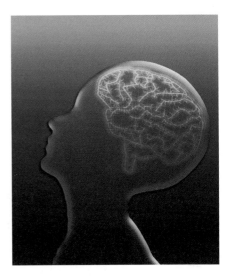

- Your personality traits or predispositions

- Your personal values and beliefs

- Your behavioral strengths and weaknesses

- Your prime motivators or drivers

- Your knowledge and skills sets

- Your experience and capabilities

All of the above elements play an important role in helping to define the person you are and also your resulting leadership style.

Understanding yourself

Over the next few pages we will explore each of these elements in turn and the interrelationships between them. We will also help you understand their potential impact on your role as a leader and, most importantly, help you determine your own strengths and possible weaknesses relating to each element.

Only when you start to explore and understand these underlying elements of personality that drive the things you do, can you then be true to yourself and become a natural and genuine leader.

Exercises

From time to time, we will suggest exercises to help you discover more about yourself. You don't need to work through all of these. Feel free to dip in to those you think may help. In addition, in Chapter 10, you'll find references to a number of online resources where you can access more in-depth information and analyses relating to various aspects of your personality.

Don't forget

It may help your understanding to attempt some of the exercises within this book. Some may need you to reflect over a number of days or even weeks in order to fully understand yourself.

Your personality

When considering your personality it is important to recognise that some elements of 'you' are relatively adaptable and, as such, can be developed relatively quickly and easily. Other aspects of your personality, however, such as your traits or predispositions are far more enduring and could, as a result, take several months or even years to change – if they can be changed at all. This is highlighted in the following diagram:

Hot tip

Be patient over trying to adapt aspects of your personality. Do not expect radical changes to the more enduring elements of your personality as this would mean changing 'you'.

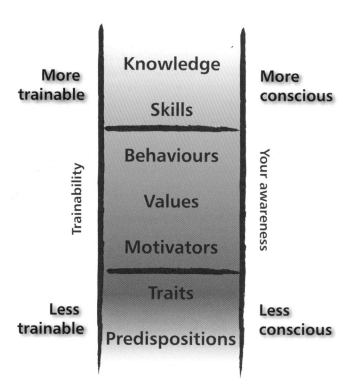

Developing not changing

The relatively enduring nature of some elements of your personality such as your personality traits or predispositions is a further reason why it's better to understand your personality and work with it rather than try to change dramatically who you are.

That is not to say that you can't change aspects of your leadership style and behaviors. You will, hopefully, see that there is still considerable scope to develop yourself to become a truly excellent and inspirational leader but you should look to adapt within the bounds of your existing personality.

Your Personality Traits

Traits defined

Right at the bottom of our chart on the previous page are traits – sometimes referred to as predispositions. Traits are generally accepted as being the most enduring characteristics of an individual's personality. Modern psychology attempts to describe personality based on what are referred to as the 'big five' traits:

Extravert	Introvert
Agreeable	**Disagreeable**
Conscientious	**Carefree**
Open	**Closed**
Emotionally controlled	**Emotionally free**

The five traits shown above are a slight adaptation of the true terms used by psychologists who generally refer to each trait by a single label. These single labels can be misleading and so ours are shown as scales with two extremes.

There is no judgement attached to either ends of these scales – there is not one end that is considered good and one end that is bad; they merely describe both ends of a continuum. It is also worth noting that it's relatively uncommon for people to be at either extremes of these scales. They are more likely to be at some point along them. Here is a brief explanation of each scale:

Extravert/Introvert

This scale is probably one of the best known of the traits and, for most, the easiest to understand. It describes the level to which people rely on the external world to gain their energy. At one extreme, *Introvert*, individuals will tend to gain their energy from within themselves. They will prefer internalizing their thoughts, prefer to relax by being on their own and will tend towards activities in work and pleasure that involve few or no other people.

Beware

Don't be judgemental about the trait profile you or others have. They define who you are so use them and play to your strengths.

At the other end of this scale, *Extrovert* describes a preference for externalizing thoughts. Extraverts will tend to gain energy by being with others. They will unwind and relax by being with others and tend towards activities that involve being with and interacting with other people. Extraverts will generally prefer to have a wider circle of friends.

Agreeable/Disagreeable
This scale describes the level to which an individual will be cooperative, sympathetic and kind towards others. If an individual is highly *Agreeable* they are likely to be affectionate, interested in other people and will generally want to strive to maintain relationships.

At the extreme of the *Disagreeable* end of this scale individuals will have little or no interest in others and are unlikely to have any particular feelings or concern for other people. They will not be concerned about maintaining relationships and therefore tend to have no worries about raising issues that may upset relationships.

Conscientious/Carefree
Here we are referring to the way individuals approach the completion of activities.

At the *Conscientious* extreme individuals will be highly self-disciplined. They will plan carefully, set in place mechanisms to ensure completion of tasks and see things through to the end. What is more, they will tend to matters of detail, ensuring everything is accurate.

The carefree end of this scale describes people who have no interest in getting things done. They will not plan but, instead, be spontaneous, preferring to live for the moment. They will have little or no interest in detail or accuracy and, when it comes to their approach to life or to completing tasks, tend to dislike organization.

Don't forget

Each end of a trait describes an extreme of the particular trait. It is more likely that you will fall at some point between these extremes.

More About Your Traits

Let's continue our descriptions of the remaining two traits:

Open/Closed

This scale describes the extent to which people are open to new ideas and experiences, to the arts and to emotions. The *Open* extreme of this scale represents individuals who will be highly inquisitive, open to new ideas and prefer thinking in conceptual terms – 'big picture' thinkers. They will be appreciative of the arts and of beauty. Open individuals enjoy and seek opportunities for variety and change.

Closed individuals are generally traditional and logical in their thinking which leaves them generally uninterested in, what they see as, frivolous distractions such as the arts. They will prefer routine and things that are straightforward and unambiguous. When considering change, they will tend to adapt existing ways, preferring incremental rather than radical change.

Being ill at ease/Emotionally free

This last scale is a difficult one because, almost by definition, the one end of the scale is seen as negative and judgemental which is not the case for the other scales. Someone who is *Ill at ease* will be emotional, negative in their thinking, anxious and highly reactive to stressful situations.

People who are *Emotionally free*, on the other hand, will be generally relaxed, comfortable with who they are, stable in terms of their moods and not easily stressed by different situations.

Beware

The *"ill at ease"* end of this scale carries with it a certain level of judgement as people do not like to think of themselves as *ill at ease*. You will therefore need to be very honest with yourself over this.

Appropriate traits

As we've already stressed, apart from the last scale, the descriptions described should not be seen to carry with them any judgement of good or bad when looked at in isolation. That said, if an individual behaves in a manner that is true to their trait, in certain situations this behavior may appear appropriate whilst, in others, inappropriate.

Take, for example, our first trait – *Introvert/Extravert.* In a situation requiring detailed analysis of a problem following careful consideration before expressing what may, perhaps, be sensitive conclusions, an individual with introvert tendencies is likely to relate quite easily to the task.

A natural introvert will be comfortable working on their own, gathering the necessary information. They will not need to verbalize their thinking and so will naturally perform this task successfully.

An extrovert, on the other hand, may be more inclined to want to verbalize their thinking as they work through the problem and this may prove highly inappropriate for the task.

Conversely, an extravert is more likely to relate and demonstrate behaviors that are appropriate to a task involving the motivation of a highly charged sales team. An introvert faced with the same task may struggle to demonstrate the most appropriate behaviors.

These two examples are, of course, rash generalizations because there are some highly introverted individuals who can still quite effectively motivate sales teams but we will explain why this is the case in the next few pages.

Adapting to The Situation

Given that we have emphasized the enduring, relatively unchanging, nature of your personality traits, you may be forgiven for thinking that there is little point in focussing any of your leadership development around this subject. What is the point in trying to understand your traits if they are so permanent?

Behaviors

Firstly, understanding your own profile and the relative strengths of each trait can help you to understand why you tend to do things the way you do; think the way you do and react the way you do. Secondly, and most importantly, whilst you naturally act based on your underlying traits, you can still choose to *behave* differently to the way your underlying profile would suggest.

If you refer to the diagram on Page 35 you'll see that behaviors, as a part of your personality profile, are slightly higher up the chart. This means they are slightly more adaptable and, at the same time, you are likely to be more conscious of them than your traits.

Preferred vs. delivered

It's important to clarify the relationship between traits and behaviors. Traits can be described as an individual's *preferred* or natural way of acting whereas behaviors are the way an individual *actually* delivers based on a given situation. Kurt Lewin, the highly respected German American psychologist, expressed this very succinctly in the following equation:

$$B = f(P \times S)$$

In other words, Behavior (B) is a function of an individual's personality traits (P) and the given situation (S) that they face.

Excellent leaders can adapt

We all tend to act based on our traits – our preferred style. Excellent leaders are able to adapt their behaviors to act in a manner that is appropriate for a given situation in order to deliver a positive outcome... even when this means behaving in a manner that's contrary to their natural trait profile.

Don't forget

You are not destined to only act and react one way because of your traits. You can learn to adapt to the situation you are facing.

Understanding your profile

Once you understand your underlying profile based on your traits you'll soon start to recognize situations or activities that play naturally to your trait profile.

More importantly, understanding your profile allows you to consciously utilize appropriate behaviors for given situations even if these behaviors are contrary to what you know to be your preferred way of behaving.

Hot tip

If you haven't already done so, try determining your trait profile so that you start to understand why you do the things you do.

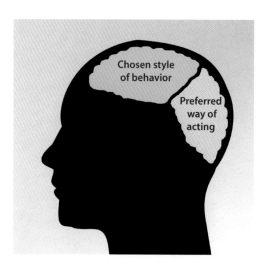

Chosen style of behavior

Preferred way of acting

41

These two statements should be seen as very liberating in terms of your future capability for delivering effectively as a leader. You do not need to think 'that's just not me'. Instead, you can think 'My natural reaction would be to do x but in this particular situation what different behaviors might I need to bring into play to achieve the desired outcome?'

Questions to ask yourself

Given what we have so far described about traits, ask yourself the following questions:

- In what situations do my traits help to deliver positive outcomes?

- In what situations are my traits likely to be unhelpful?

- In what situations do I need to consider adapting my behaviors?

Behaviors Hold The Key

Highly successful leaders develop behaviors that can support and deliver exceptional outcomes even where their natural traits don't necessarily align with the required activity.

These behaviors may themselves have developed and become reinforced over many years – possibly dating back to childhood experiences. As a result, you should not be surprised if some of your behaviors take several months or, perhaps, even years to adapt to a point where they become natural to you.

Raising your consciousness

Once you start to explore some of the behaviors described in the rest of this chapter you will no doubt begin to recognize those which you already demonstrate. You may feel others are ones you need to develop or learn to manage.

We will explore more about how you can develop or manage those behaviors in which you are weaker, later in this chapter. For now, just understanding each of the behaviors and their potential impact on the outcomes of your leadership actions will start to raise your consciousness of your own behavioral profile.

Competence and competencies

Just a short note of clarification. Some organizations develop what are often referred to as 'competency frameworks'. In this context the term 'competencies' is often another way of describing behaviors. This, however, is very different to 'competence' which is a measure of whether an individual has the right knowledge and skills to be deemed competent to do the job.

Hot tip

The key to working with and developing behaviors is to firstly raise your awareness of your own behavioral profile.

Typical behaviors

There are many behavioral or competency frameworks used by organizations, all of which will slice the 'behavioral cake' slightly differently. Over the next few pages we have described just one way of defining a range of leadership behaviors. You'll see our behaviors have been grouped into four main clusters or themes:

THINKING	DELIVERY
Analytical thinking	Focus on achievement
Strategic thinking	Attention to detail
Conceptual thinking	Tenacity
Client-oriented thinking	Concern for excellence

RELATIONSHIPS	SELF-MANAGEMENT
Interpersonal awareness	Resilience
Adaptive behavior	Self-development
Stakeholder relationships	Self-control
Influencing/persuading	Self-confidence

Beware

Whilst we describe here a typical set of behaviors, you may come across slightly different versions used within your organization - this is understandable given the complexity and intangible nature of behaviors.

43

Self-analysis

Over the next few pages we'll explore each of the above clusters in turn and the behaviors within each one. As you read through the brief outlines for each behavior, try to think back to situations where you have demonstrated the described behaviors.

Keep a note of those behaviors you feel you are strong in and those where you believe you are not so strong. It may help to rank yourself on a scale of, say, 0-4 where 0 represents no or little evidence of you delivering the behavior and 4 represents strong or frequent use of the behavior.

Thinking Behaviors

The first behaviors we are going to describe relate to the way you think. We are going to consider four very distinct elements of thinking.

Analytical Thinking

Analytical Thinking, as its name suggests, describes a form of thinking relating to the analysis of situations or problems and the drawing of conclusions from the resultant data.

This involves focussing on detail, systematically breaking down an issue into its constituent elements or back to its root cause. A leader who is a strong analytical thinker will evaluate the pros and cons of a range of options, test in their mind the reliability of the data supplied and apply logic to any decision-making process.

Analytical thinkers can therefore be described as people who generally focus on detail and data.

Hot tip

As you read through these descriptions, if you find one difficult to relate to or understand it may be because you don't naturally demonstrate the described behavior.

Conceptual Thinking

Conceptual Thinking is very different to analytical thinking in that it is concerned with a breadth of thinking – of patterns or possible connections between what may sometimes appear unrelated ideas or occurrences. This time the interest in data relates to how they fit together as part of a big picture rather than the detail of the individual items.

Leaders who are conceptual thinkers are, as a result, likely to focus on developing new ideas, thinking about broader, higher level issues and may therefore be more creative and possibly artistic.

Strategic Thinking

Thinking strategically involves being able to visualize the future – applying thinking to the long-term direction of a problem or function. Strategic thinkers focus initially on the end goals or outcomes rather than on the shorter-term tactics.

Leaders who are strong strategic thinkers will often tend to reinforce their thinking with *Analytical Thinking* in order to validate their plans as well as *Conceptual Thinking* to ensure they take into account the broader issues on which the strategy is likely to be based.

Client-oriented Thinking

This category of thinking relates to how empathetic an individual is relating to the client or customer (whether they are an internal or external customer) and their needs.

A strong client-oriented leader will naturally understand and consider the client's requirements, priorities and perspective and will apply their thinking based on that client perspective.

Combining thinking behaviors

You will hopefully see already (especially if you are a strong conceptual thinker!) that behaviors do not sit in isolation. They can each combine to provide subtly different outcomes. A strong client-oriented thinker who is also a strategic thinker, for instance, is likely to develop a long-term vision that has the client right at the center of that strategy.

Don't forget

None of the described behaviors works in isolation. Try to understand how each of them interacts with and impacts others described over the next few pages.

45

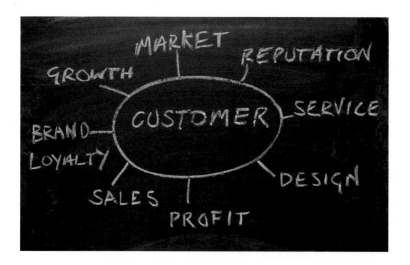

Delivering Results Behaviors

Leaders who excel at making things happen will consistently demonstrate one or more of the behaviors described below:

Focus on achievement

Individuals strong in this behavior will naturally put in place goals, objectives or milestones that focus on achieving a desired outcome. Excellent leaders demonstrating this behavior will plan; define actions; allocate resources but also set in place measures and then monitor to ensure that the plan is delivered.

Leaders with this behavior not only set clear standards for themselves but also for others. All of their focus and actions will be concerned with achieving the intended goal.

Don't forget

Ultimately, leadership is about getting things done and therefore these behaviors are critical for any leader.

Attention to detail

The name of this behavior is self-explanatory. Individuals who are strong in this behavior will be thorough, accurate and concerned with seeing things through to completion.

Leaders strong in this behavior tend to plan meticulously, ensuring that all details are taken into account, whereas those with low attention to detail are only likely to deal with things on a very cursory level.

Combining other behaviors

As well as combining behaviors within clusters, many behaviors from different clusters combine or support each other in ways that define an individual's unique behavioral profile. Take, for instance, *Attention to Detail* and *Analytical Thinking*. These two behaviors, when combined, deliver an overall behavioral profile that supports a leader who needs to be involved in detailed processes and planning. A very different profile results if the leader is less analytical but instead is strong in *Conceptual Thinking*.

Concern for excellence

This behavior is concerned with setting and striving for high standards. When this behavior is combined with *Focus on Achievement* this is likely to deliver excellence in terms of the final result. Conversely, if demonstrated by a leader with little interest delivering the behavior *Focus on Achievement*, this *Concern for Excellence* may be directed towards excellence over the method of delivery rather than in the end result.

Striving for perfection can be a strength for a leader but, if taken to an extreme and not balanced with a level of *Focus on Achievement* leaders may not complete tasks on time due to them never being quite satisfied with the result.

Tenacity

For many leadership situations *Tenacity* can be a useful behavior. Leaders must not give up too easily but be prepared to persevere in order to see things through to a conclusion. Tenacity may be particularly needed when faced with opposition, challenging circumstances or when having to deal with setbacks.

Beware

Extremes of any behavior can be a drawback rather than a help as is the case if someone is so bothered about achieving perfection that they never finish the work.

Of course, as with most behaviors, there can also be a negative side. In this case being too tenacious – perhaps putting over an argument and not recognizing when it may be more appropriate to the overall outcome to back down or let go.

47

Relationships Behaviors

A critical element of any leadership role is the ability to engage with and get the very best out of people. It is not surprising, therefore, that the following behaviors relating to relationships are all very important:

Interpersonal Awareness

Interpersonal awareness is about observing and having a understanding for others' feelings and motives. An individual who is strong in this behavior will be conscious not only of what another person is saying but also the subtleties in the way it is expressed and the body language being put over. As a result, they will most likely have a far deeper empathy for what the individual is trying to convey – far beyond just what is being said.

Adaptive Behavior

In a way, *Adaptive Behavior* complements *Interpersonal Awareness* as this behavior is about the way an individual consciously modifies their approach or behavior in order to meet the needs of the situation or the needs of the other person. It is only truly possible to do this with reasonable levels of *Interpersonal Awareness* in the first place.

Hot tip

Part of *Interpersonal Awareness* is about being able to interpret body language – a subject we will come back to in Chapter 3.

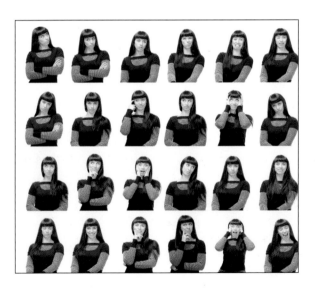

An individual demonstrating low or no *Adaptive Behavior* is likely to interact with others based on a single, possibly inappropriate, style of delivery. They may be oblivious to, or unconcerned with, the impact of their style of delivery.

Stakeholder Relationships

This behavior is more than just blindly developing business relationships with others. It is concerned with strategically identifying and building business relationships that will be of benefit to you, the organization or for a specific piece of work.

Excellent leaders systematically identify people from a variety of positions or backgrounds – whether political, cultural or hierarchical – who they believe can influence the outcome of their activities. They will consider alternative influencing tactics, where necessary, to gain the appropriate level of support.

Beware

Don't just 'collect' business cards and think you are effectively networking. Your networking connections need to be based on relevance to you and your work.

Influencing/persuading

It's important to distinguish here between techniques and processes for influencing, these being learnt skills, and *Influencing* as a behavior. As a behavior we are concerned with an individual's concern to present arguments in a logical and persuasive manner.

Individuals demonstrating high levels of this behavior will look for areas of mutual interest in order to persuade. They will use data to reinforce their viewpoint and focus on factual evidence rather than on emotional tactics.

Where this behavior is combined with *Analytical Thinking*, an individual is likely to focus on detailed data in order to support their case. Where, on the other hand, an individual is a strong conceptual thinker, they are likely to use broader-based arguments based on their conceptual logic.

Self-Management Behaviors

This cluster of behaviors is arguably the most important of all those we have described. Being able to manage yourself is critical to your success as a leader.

Resilience

Excellent leaders are able to stand up to difficult situations and are not demotivated when faced with setbacks. They will be determined to achieve goals or outcomes even when faced with significant opposition.

When combined with *Interpersonal Relationships*, individuals will also tend to assess others' reactions to their position or argument and, as a result, be sensitive to the impact of their stance. Resilience should not, of course, be confused with stubbornness.

Self-development

Just the fact that you are reading this book is an indication that you can demonstrate some level of this behavior. This is good news because there is a strong correlation between individuals who take their personal development seriously and successful leadership.

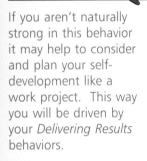

Hot tip

If you aren't naturally strong in this behavior it may help to consider and plan your self-development like a work project. This way you will be driven by your *Delivering Results* behaviors.

50

Individuals strong in this behavior take responsibility for their personal development. They will have a clear understanding of their development and career goals and actively seek opportunities to expand their roles and experiences to meet these goals. They will constantly evaluate their own performance and see all experiences as development opportunities.

Self-control

It is important, especially when dealing with sensitive situations, for a leader to be in control of their emotions – not losing their temper or, on the other hand, becoming over-excited.

Individuals who demonstrate high levels of *Self-control* will be conscious of the way they would normally react, especially under stressful situations or if provoked, and will tend to portray a more controlled response to a situation, when needed. This will be especially true where they also demonstrate high levels of *Adaptive Behavior.*

Of course, an extreme level of *Self-control* could lead to an individual coming across as cold and unexpressive which, for a leader, is likely to be unhelpful.

Self-Confidence

Leaders must believe in their own capability to lead, to make decisions and in the work they do. This self-confidence comes from a heightened understanding of their personal strengths and weaknesses. Any lack of self-confidence is so easily picked up by others and so can undermine a leader's credibility.

Individuals who demonstrate self-confidence will have a 'can-do' attitude when approaching tasks but, at the same time, will be realistic about their capabilities. They will not worry about taking on challenges or additional responsibilities but will only do so on the basis of a balanced appreciation of their capability to deliver.

Beware

Having a level of Self-control can be useful but watch that this doesn't lead to you coming across as unexpressive.

Personal Values

Moving on from behaviors we will now turn to another important element of your personality profile – your personal values. Again, you will need to explore and understand these in terms of your own profile so that you can ensure you remain true to yourself as a successful leader.

Rule book

Your values or beliefs can be considered as your personal internal rule book by which you live your life and make decisions and judgements. Most of the time you make decisions without having to consciously refer to your values. Values are more adaptable than your traits or behaviors but even so, you are unlikely to change them unless you consciously choose to question their validity.

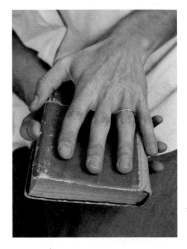

Referring to the diagram on Page 35 you will therefore note that values sit in the middle of our diagram.

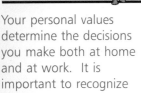

Don't forget

Your personal values determine the decisions you make both at home and at work. It is important to recognize that not everyone has the same beliefs and personal values.

Values and beliefs may include religious beliefs but also many others relating to all aspects of your life. For example your:

- Political beliefs

- Feelings towards helping others

- Beliefs about justice and fairness

- Beliefs about religion – in general and also specific religions

- Attitudes towards your education and learning

- Reactions to obeying rules

- Values relating to honesty

- Preferences regarding job satisfaction

- Values relating to freedom of expression

Sometimes irrational

The examples listed on the previous page are just a few of the more obvious values. Values can sometimes be quite irrational when based, perhaps, on a childhood incident or piece of early parental advice.

An individual may, for example, subconsciously always avoid painting rooms green purely based on a single bad experience relating to a green room when they were a child.

Understanding personal values

Most of the decisions you make, based on your personal values, are done sub-consciously. Therefore, if you are to understand your values and how they inform your thinking, you will initially need to raise them to a more conscious level. To help you do this we suggest you try the following exercise:

Values Exercise

In Chapter 10 we have provided a listing of some of the more common values. Take a good look through the list and note the ones that are important for you. If there are others not listed, you can add some of your own.

From the list, try to choose just your top ten most important values in terms of drivers within your leadership role. Then try expanding the single word prompts into more meaningful statements. For instance, you may have chosen the word *"Independence"* and from this your expanded statement may be: *"I feel it is important that those working for me are able to feel a level of independence and space to work based on their own style of operation"*.

Thinking about each of these statements can help you be clearer about your own values and how they impact the way you act as a leader. Be prepared to challenge some of your values if you start to notice they are unhelpful or irrational.

Hot tip

It can be quite enlightening to consciously consider some of your values and to question what has led you to determine that these are right for you.

When looking to develop yourself, focus on maximizing your strengths more than minimizing your weaknesses.

Your Overall Leadership Style

There is an old adage 'Maximize your strengths and minimise your weaknesses'. This isn't so far off the mark but you will probably find you can gain more from developing one of your strengths by 5% than you will from improving one of your weaknesses by 30-40%. What is more, you are likely to be far more motivated about developing a strength further, than you will be by focussing on a weakness, for which you may have little interest.

Remember our key message is about being yourself rather than trying to emulate someone else. In this context, what we are suggesting here is that you focus on being more of yourself – the best elements, that is.

Analyzing your own personality

If you haven't already done so, take a look back through the different elements of personality described in this chapter. Determine where you would position yourself for each of the five traits. Remember that there is no judgement attached to either end of the trait scales.

Similarly, look through the behaviors we've described and determine how strong you are in demonstrating each of the sixteen behaviors. You may find it useful to use the scales shown on the opposite page.

Place a mark at a point along each scale where '0' represents having no understanding or where you believe you never demonstrate any aspects of the behavior and '10' represents you believe you frequently or strongly demonstrate the given behavior.

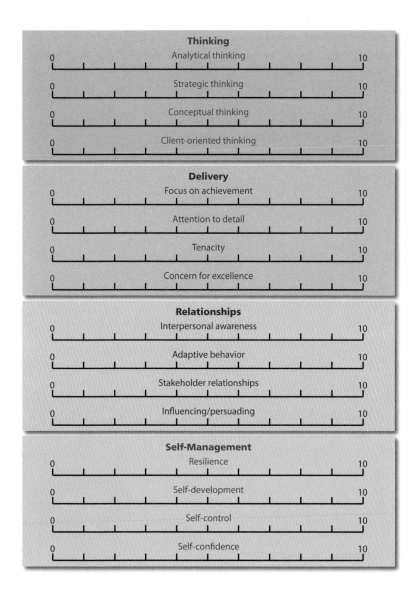

Thinking

Analytical thinking
0 ——————————————— 10

Strategic thinking
0 ——————————————— 10

Conceptual thinking
0 ——————————————— 10

Client-oriented thinking
0 ——————————————— 10

Delivery

Focus on achievement
0 ——————————————— 10

Attention to detail
0 ——————————————— 10

Tenacity
0 ——————————————— 10

Concern for excellence
0 ——————————————— 10

Relationships

Interpersonal awareness
0 ——————————————— 10

Adaptive behavior
0 ——————————————— 10

Stakeholder relationships
0 ——————————————— 10

Influencing/persuading
0 ——————————————— 10

Self-Management

Resilience
0 ——————————————— 10

Self-development
0 ——————————————— 10

Self-control
0 ——————————————— 10

Self-confidence
0 ——————————————— 10

Beware

It is unlikely you will be at the extremes of many (if any) of the scales shown. Try to compare how strong you are in each behavior relative to the others.

55

Independent and professional guidance

Whilst you may be able to gain an insight into your behavioral profile from the descriptions we've provided, you may benefit from receiving a more structured and thorough analysis either by completing an appropriate psychometric assessment or by receiving personal feedback following a behavioral or competency-based interview.

You will find some useful reference material and resources on this subject in Chapter 10.

Hot tip

You may be able to ask some of your closest work colleagues to give you feedback about behaviors in which you feel you need help.

Managing The Gaps

Of course you may not be able to merely ignore your weaknesses. You may, for example, become aware of a weakness in your overall leadership profile you believe is causing you difficulties. You may discover this from a number of sources:

- You become conscious that particular situations or activities are proving difficult for you to deal with

- Others give you feedback on your actions relating to certain situations

- Your results relating to some of your leadership activities are not as you want them to be

- You become aware of weaknesses from reading this book or from professional feedback following the completion of psychometric or personality exercises

However you first become aware of a particular weakness, you should start by asking yourself:

- How important is it for me to address this weakness?

- What would be the consequences of not doing anything about it?

- What alternatives could I consider to tackle this?

- Is this a short-term problem or is it likely to recur?

For example, you may be concerned that you don't tend to notice minor inaccuracies in pieces of work. This may be as a result of your trait profile being more towards the *Carefree* end of our scale rather than *Conscientious* and also being lower in the related behavior *Attention to Detail*.

Asking the above questions can help you to determine whether this is a short-term issue due to workload pressures or something that is likely to keep recurring and therefore in need of addressing.

Managing the behavior

Before jumping into a development activity in an attempt to strengthen a behavior, take a look at all the available options. For instance, rather than attempting to change a behavior – something that could take a considerable amount of time and effort – how about looking at ways to *manage* it instead?

Look at alternatives

In our example, what systems or forms of alternative support could you put in place to ensure that issues relating to detail get picked up and checked? You could, for example:

- Set aside one hour per week specifically to slow down and focus on dealing with issues requiring detail

- Develop some form of reminder to encourage you to look at the detail

- Acknowledge your weakness and ensure that someone else always oversees your work to provide a final check when it comes to dealing with issues of detail

Hot tip

It may be more fruitful to consider ways to manage a weaker behavior rather than trying to develop it from scratch.

57

Development options

In Chapter 9 we will explore ideas relating to your personal development and, should you decide you still need to focus on developing one of your weaker behaviors, we will help you determine a range of suitable development actions.

Summary

We have covered a lot of ground in this chapter on a wide range of important aspects of your leadership style. Let's recap some of the main points:

- Don't try to copy other leaders' styles because their styles will only work for them based on their underlying personality profiles – learn to just be yourself and focus on developing your own leadership style based on your personality

- Develop a strong sense of trust between you and those that work with you. If you want them to trust you, start by learning to have trust in them and their capabilities

- Some elements of your personality, such as traits and behaviors are relatively stable and you'll therefore be less conscious of them. To develop an understanding of these aspects of your personality you will firstly need to develop an awareness of them

- Your personal values provide you with your unconscious rule book by which you run your life and make decisions

- It is generally accepted that your personality is made up of the 'big five' traits. While each trait has descriptors for each end of its scale, neither is deemed to be good or bad – they are just more appropriate for different roles and situations

- Your behavior is a function of your traits and the situation you are experiencing. As a leader you need to learn to adapt your behaviors to support the situation you are facing

- Organizations each define behaviors or competencies slightly differently but critically, you should look to strengthen and utilize those behaviors that support your leadership activity

- It may help to seek external and independent help in order to better understand your personality and behavioral profiles

- When considering how you develop your behavioral profile it may be better to focus on strengthening your strong behaviors further rather than just focussing on your weaker ones

- You may be able to find alternative ways of supporting or managing your weaker behaviors rather than having to necessarily develop them

3 Empowering People

Excellent leaders empower individuals and teams so that those working for them feel the same sense of responsibility for their work as the leader. Much of this is down to the organizational climate and the way people are engaged and trusted.

You Can't Do It All Yourself

Let's say you decide to start a new business and at first it's just you developing your new product or service. Of course, at the same time you will also need to be out there finding potential buyers and suppliers, handling the PR, coming up with the promotional material and sorting out your IT system and website.

That may be fine for the first few months or so but, as a result of your early success, you will probably soon realize you just can't cope with demand and so you decide to take on your first employee. Firstly, congratulations, you are now a leader! Now you have others working with you, you'll need to allocate work and responsibilities between you and you will also need to start sharing your vision for the business.

Of course, for many it's not about starting a new business – they are already a part of, or are recruited into, an existing organization with, perhaps, hundreds if not thousands of employees.

Letting go

Whatever is the situation for you, the message is the same – there is no point having other people working for you if you're not prepared to let go of some of the work.

This sounds so blindingly obvious and yet so many leaders do not, in practice, seem to understand this. Instead, they run around trying to:

- Do everything

- Be in touch with all the latest management data

- Measure everything

- Come up with all the ideas

As a result, these leaders hold back their organization or at least the part of the organization they are responsible for, stifling the creativity of those that work for them.

This problem can often be seen with inexperienced managers who are reluctant to let go, either because they haven't learnt how to delegate effectively or because they're under the misunderstanding that to do everything puts them in a position of power.

In reality, nothing could be further from the truth. Taking on all the work and all the responsibility leaves you with little or no time to focus on the true leadership aspects of your role such as strategic planning and, more importantly, leading people.

Those in your team lose

Probably the biggest loss resulting from a leader not being prepared to let go is the impact it will have on the climate for those working under the leader. You may want to refer back to the questions we posed on Page 18 regarding climate.

When a leader is too heavily involved in doing the work, individuals are likely to feel distrusted, de-valued and unclear about their role in delivering the objectives of the organization.

Worse still, instead of feeling empowered and responsible for their part of the process or business, they are likely to pull back and either wait for the leader to come up with the solutions or try to second guess what they believe the leader would want done instead of coming up with their own fresh ideas.

Beware

Not letting go of work is likely to have a very negative impact on the organization. People will feel a lack of involvement and trust.

61

You lose

What we have not so far described in this situation is the impact it is likely to have on you, your health and your sanity. If you are unable to let go of work, there is no way you can keep up with the work output of even a small-sized team, let alone a larger-sized team or organization.

Very quickly you are likely to become tired, ineffective and this could potentially lead to you burning yourself out and not being able to keep up.

Encouraging Responsibility

Your leadership style

As a leader you must choose – and, critically, it is a choice – whether to be 'directive' in your leadership style and approach to a given situation or more 'hands-off'. The following diagram describes the two ends of this leadership styles continuum:

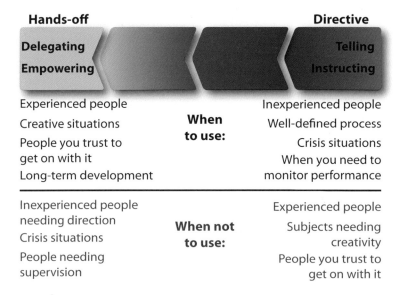

Hands-off		Directive
Delegating Empowering		Telling Instructing

	When to use:	
Experienced people		Inexperienced people
Creative situations		Well-defined process
People you trust to get on with it		Crisis situations
Long-term development		When you need to monitor performance

	When not to use:	
Inexperienced people needing direction		Experienced people
Crisis situations		Subjects needing creativity
People needing supervision		People you trust to get on with it

Hot tip

Think about what style of leadership you generally adopt. Are you more directive or hands-off? There is a time and situation for both but generally you should use a more hands-off style.

62

You will see that provided you are dealing with individuals who are experienced, the most appropriate style is hands-off. Only where you have inexperienced people or if facing a crisis situation are you likely to need to resort to a more directive style.

Preferred style

Most leaders want to develop individuals and teams that are engaged, committed and (other than in the few situations indicated) able and prepared to take responsibility for their work. It is encouraging this engagement and sense of responsibility that's at the heart of empowering people. You will hopefully see that this is more likely to be achieved where the leader adopts a hands-off style of leadership rather than a directive style.

Whilst ultimate responsibility will probably need to remain with the leader, in many cases it is beneficial for those involved in the delivery to assume responsibility for their work. In so doing they will take pride in their achievements knowing these have been the result of their hard work not just as a result of following orders.

Responsibility for what?

When referring to taking responsibility we are not just referring to responsibility for delivering a defined outcome. If a leader is working in a truly hands-off style, the individual or team should be encouraged to take responsibility for:

- Defining what the final outcome is expected to be

- Determining the measures of success

- Determining the best methodology for delivering the outcome

- Monitoring and reporting progress

- Revising the methodology where necessary in order to bring a piece of work back on track

- Celebrating success and evaluating the learning from the experience

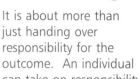

Don't forget

It is about more than just handing over responsibility for the outcome. An individual can take on responsibility for all these aspects of a piece of work.

A time for direction

The above is the ideal and, as suggested in our diagram, should be possible if you are dealing with more experienced individuals or teams who you can trust to take on this sort of responsibility. Leaving a relatively inexperienced individual with the same level of responsibility, on the other hand, could leave the individual unskilled and feeling unsupported and lost.

Moving towards a hands-off style

If you have not previously been using a hands-off style with an individual you may find the first time you attempt it, the individual tries to push the responsibility back to you. Rather than accept this, encourage them to take more of the responsibility. Initially it may help to just give them responsibility for the outcomes of a piece of work but over time encourage them to take more responsibility for more of the aspects listed above.

Clarity of Mission

How clearly does your team understand the overall purpose or mission of your team or the organization? More importantly, how well do they understand the *linkages* between their roles and the organization's mission?

You may have a very busy team but, without clarity over how their work impacts and supports the delivery of the overall mission they cannot be expected to align their work in a way in which they can effectively deliver the mission.

Deep understanding

Clarity of mission is so much more than just being able to recite, verbatim, a set of statements about what the organization is and what it is set up to achieve. It's about a far deeper – even emotional – understanding by all individuals, of the organization's purpose and their role in delivering it. If change is needed to deliver the outputs or goals of the organization, individuals should know what they will need to do differently within their roles in order to deliver this change.

Hot tip

Don't just rely on job descriptions to explain people's roles. Ensure that you regularly discuss with the them the links between their roles and the strategic business plans.

64

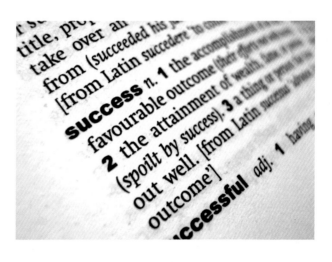

Recognizing success

Every person in the team, whatever their role, needs to understand the overall direction and what success will look like for the organization as a whole and within their own role. Without this understanding, individuals will not be able to apply themselves in a meaningful way. Instead they will merely perform a set of activities in a vacuum, with no personal commitment to the overall outcome.

Communicating a Vision

There are many leaders who consider themselves to be visionaries – believing they are capable of coming up with inpirational new ideas for their organizations. But in reality, are these ideas just a series of random tactics for how things could be done better? Or, on the other hand, are they truly visionary ideas that map out the road ahead and describe the coherent long-term strategic direction for the organization?

Even if the latter is the case, is the leader capable of translating this vision with sufficient clarity that those required to deliver the vision truly understand the leader's ideas?

It's about inspiration
Even when a leader provides direction and is able to express it clearly, is it delivered with enthusiasm and energy? Are people inspired and fully committed to making it work?

Ownership
You are far more likely to obtain the level of commitment suggested here if individuals feel fully 'bought in' to the vision. One way to develop a sense of ownership is to involve people in the development of the vision. Instead of merely imposing your own vision, ask others for their perspectives, seek their input and keep them involved throughout its development.

Translating into personal goals
The same applies when focussing on an individual's personal goals or objectives. If they are fully committed to the vision and they have clarity over their part in achieving it they will naturally want to set their own personal goals with minimal involvement needed from you as their leader.

Don't forget

It's not just what you say but the way that you say it. Ensure you are enthusiastic about the vision and express this when you are discussing it with others.

Effective Delegation

As this book is about leadership and not management, we are not focussing on the processes involved when delegating but looking instead at how, through delegation, you can empower people and engender a real sense of responsibility within the individual.

Management perspective

If viewing delegation from a purely management perspective the main considerations are:

- Who is the most appropriate person to delegate to with the appropriate skills and who you can trust?

- How can tasks and responsibilities be shared fairly to ensure everyone in the team is equally or appropriately employed?

- How can activities be allocated to help develop individuals?

Leadership perspective

These considerations are important from the perspective of managing a task but as a leader your focus is more likely to be:

- How can delegating help to build confidence and a sense of responsibility in an individual?

- How can delegating this responsibility help to engender a sense of ownership to the overall mission?

- Does the individual understand how this activity contributes to the overall purpose and how does it therefore help them to understand their role within the context of the bigger picture?

You will see that the emphasis is more towards the longer-term benefits to the individual and the organization.

Don't forget

Delegation is about so much more than just passing a task onto someone. Use delegation as a way of developing greater responsibilty.

Wider appreciation

Taking time to jointly explore the nature of an activity and, in particular, how the activity contributes to the bigger picture will ultimately encourage the individual to take more responsibility and to understand more about the part that their role plays within the overall organizational machine. With this wider appreciation individuals are more likely to understand and fully commit to the activity being delegated.

Engendering trust

Effective delegation is about letting go of the ownership of an activity to truly pass on the responsibility to the receiving individual. Wherever possible you should be looking to pass on not only responsibility for the ultimate outcome but also for determining the method of delivery.

If you are able to do this the messages that this sends out to the individual regarding your trust in them and their capabilities will be extremely positive.

If you have not done so before, letting go of responsibility for determining the method of delivery can be quite a challenge. There is a danger you will be tempted to jump in and offer suggestions – either at the outset or when the individual hits their first difficulties. This may be for truly positive reasons such as your wish to see the individual succeed, but this is likely to undermine any messages of trust you may have created.

Supporting behaviors

Based on the behavioral descriptions we described in Chapter 2, leaders who delegate effectively will be supported by behaviors such as *Strategic Thinking* in terms of considering the longer-term position and generally the behaviors within the *Delivering Results* cluster, although if these are too strong, the leader is more likely to want to personally achieve than delegate this to others.

Most importantly, from the *Relationships* cluster, behaviors such as *Interpersonal Awareness* support effective delegation because this ensures the leader is able to gauge the reactions of the individual to the activity being delegated. You might think that *Influencing/ Persuading* would also support effective delegation but care needs to be taken that the individual doesn't feel led or sold into the idea of taking on the activity.

Hot tip

Refer back to the behaviors which you are strong in. Think about whether they naturally support your ability to delegate effectively?

Learning to Listen

How much time do you spend truly listening to what your people are saying? The sign of an excellent leader is that they are not afraid to spend time truly listening to:

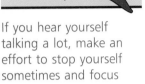
68

- Ideas people may have to improve the organization and the way it functions

- Feedback on how things are going and the climate people are experiencing

- Feedback on the leader's own performance

- Rumours, gossip, 'word-on-the-street' discussion amongst employees

This last one may appear a little odd to include but by being alert to what is being spread within an organization via the 'grapevine' a good leader can get an excellent insight into the issues concerning people across the organization and hence the climate.

Asking questions

A confident leader is not afraid to ask questions and, most importantly, they are not afraid to listen to the responses! The impact that this has in terms of building trust and engagement can be extremely powerful. You are effectively saying: "Whilst I'm the leader, I am not pretending to know all the answers and I value your viewpoint and experience".

Of course, this should not just be done for effect. People can tell whether you are truly open to their suggestions and comments.

Needless to say, one of the most critical behaviors supporting effective listening has to be *Interpersonal Awareness*. But this behavior is far more than merely listening.

Body language

What is transmitted by the words people say is but a small fraction of the overall message being communicated. Commonly quoted research by Albert Mehrabian from the 1970s suggests the following levels of impact for various aspects of communication:

- 7% is communicated via the actual words spoken

- 38% is communicated through tone of voice

- 55% is communicated through body language

So to truly listen to what people are saying, we need to focus on the 93% of communication that's transmitted other than through the words themselves. Just from looking at the following facial expressions you can interpret a lot of what is meant:

Beware

Don't just focus on the words being said. There is much more than just the words being communicated. Tune into the subtleties of what is really inferred.

69

Avoid pigeon-holing

As experienced leaders, we tend to listen for similarities in what we hear so that we can label and deal with the issue based on similar previous situations. After all, this can save a lot of time and effort, especially if we found an acceptable solution last time.

Unfortunately, once we find a close enough match we tend to switch off from listening effectively. This is a great pity because this is when we start to miss out on the subtle differences in what is really being said. Force yourself to truly listen to what people are trying to put over when communicating with you.

Trusting Others

We have already touched on the issue of trust and in particular its impact on organizational climate. If you are to empower people so that they feel truly engaged and responsible for both the method of delivery and the outcomes, you must have – and must demonstrate – total trust in them and their capabilities to deliver.

Having belief in their capability to deliver, however, is only one half of demonstrating trust. The other half is communicated through your willingness to let go of activities or areas of responsibility. If you know an individual has the capability to deliver but you are still reluctant to let go, the message that is sent out can seriously undermine the sense of trust you're attempting to build and convey.

Capability

Of course, there will be times when you choose to delegate an activity to an individual to stretch them or where, perhaps, they need experience but have not yet proven their capability. Demonstrating your trust in them may just help give them the confidence they need.

Safety net

This is a good use of delegation but under these circumstances it may still be appropriate to offer a 'safety net' to the individual to give them a feeling of security whilst also allowing them the freedom to work through their own solutions.

If you're not prepared to let go but instead feel the need to lead the individual every step of the way, you won't give them the space and confidence to work it out for themselves and so they will continue to remain reliant on you to make all the decisions.

Hot tip

Just offering to be there in case they need help can be enough to give someone the confidence needed to take on new responsibilities.

Monitoring progress

When delegating an activity or responsibility, especially for the first time, you'll no doubt want to keep a close eye on progress, if only to ensure the individual is coping and making progress. Monitoring too closely, though, might appear to be intrusive and suggest a lack of trust in their capability.

Ask them

One of the best ways to deal with this is to ask the individual up front how they would want you to keep a track of progress. Explain that you want to offer support and ensure they are not left to fail.

Ideally, provided the climate is positive in the first place and they have therefore accepted the responsibility positively, they are more likely to want to monitor their own progress and report this to you without you needing to check up on them yourself. Alternatively, they may at least give you the green light to monitor them but this still leaves the control with the individual.

Demonstrating trust

Here are some other ways in which you can demonstrate your trust in individuals and teams:

- Look at your employee policies and consider the messages they infer relating to trust. Do you really need, for example, to have clocking in and out procedures?

- When you allocate responsibilities, do you tend to always favour certain individuals and ignore others?

- Where you do need to provide direction, try recommending rather than imposing direction

Hot tip

Actively look for opportunities to demonstrate your trust in people – it can make a big difference to your relationships with them.

Others' Trust in You

Trust is a two way street. Those that work for you need to feel they can trust you to:

- Be there when they need you

- Do what you say you'll do

- Let them work without unnecessary interference from you

- Not look to blame or criticize them if they make a mistake (initially)

Making mistakes

This last point, which we highlighted a little earlier, is an important one from the perspective of developing a climate of trust and empowerment. When taking on new responsibilities or activities for the first time, people inevitably make mistakes – unless, that is, you hold their hand every step of the way. This needs to be seen as part of the learning process as opposed to an opportunity to highlight their lack of capability.

Beware

When someone makes a mistake, stop yourself from immediately jumping in and taking over or looking to criticize. Take a step back and ask them to analyze what happened.

72

If individuals believe, when they are first given a piece of work, that they are being set up to fail or that they will be penalized for trying and failing, then it is highly unlikely that they'll be prepared to take on new responsibilities willingly.

Of course, where an individual has been given appropriate development and support and continues to fail then there may be cause for some form of intervention.

Being a Sounding Board

Providing that a positive climate of trust has been established, individuals should feel confident to call on you when needed to test out their thinking and to gain reassurance when needing to make difficult or challenging decisions.

Beyond just a sounding board

Without undermining an individual's sense of responsibility it can sometimes be useful to test or challenge their thinking or a proposed course of action. Provided this is done in a positive and constructive way, you can help them to set in place the right sort of processes so that in future they can have more confidence in their own decisions. Depending on the nature of the subject being discussed, challenging questions you could ask might be:

- What other options did/could you explore?

- How confident are you over what you are proposing?

- How realistic are you about succeeding with this course of action?

- What additional help do you think you'll need with this?

You will note that none of these questions are meant to be either judgemental or undermining – they are just designed to help the individual to think through all angles.

Leading questions

If you are merely acting as a sounding board you need to remain neutral in your questioning and certainly avoid questions that push an individual in a particular direction such as: "Are you sure it wouldn't be better to follow an alternative path such as...?" Leading questions such as this take the control back from the individual and undermine their sense of responsibility.

Hot tip

There are many questions you can ask which will help test the thinking of the individual but always watch they don't become leading.

Summary

- Excellent leaders do not try to know everything, do everything and come up with all the ideas. Instead, they empower others to take true responsibility for aspects of the delivery

- Leaders have a choice whether to be directive in their approach or whether to be more hands-off. It is far more likely to engender responsibility in individuals and teams if the leader can work towards a hands-off style

- When handing over responsibility to others it is best if the leader hands over responsibility for not only the outcome but also for how to get there and the evaluation of success

- For people to be able to truly engage with the organization they need to understand the organization's mission and, most importantly, how their role contributes towards that mission

- Being a visionary is fine but an excellent leader also needs to be able to communicate the vision to those who will be responsible for delivering it

- An important change for many leaders when trying to empower people is to do less talking and more listening. This way people start to feel their contribution is valued

- Trust is one of the most fundamental elements of empowerment – trust by the leader in his or her people as well as the trust by people in their leader

- Trust is about letting go and believing in people. This can be difficult to do if, as a leader, you have previously held on to responsibilities

- When people try things for the first time the leader can provide confidence by offering to be there as a 'safety net'

- People need to feel that they can have the freedom to try things out and if they make the odd mistake in the process, they won't be blamed or criticized

- Without needing to provide explicit direction a leader can play an important role just by offering to be there as a sounding board when individuals need reassurance

4 Valuing Others' Views

Being a leader does not mean having a monopoly on all the good ideas. Successful leaders actively seek and use a wide range of ideas and the different perspectives of those around them.

More Than One Perspective

Over the years you will have no doubt come up with many good ideas and made very many business decisions. Hopefully many of these ideas and decisions have worked out well – for you and your organization. That said, it would be difficult to imagine that during this time you have not also come up with some ideas that did not turn out to be so bright or made a few decisions that turned out to be wrong.

Before coming up with your ideas or making these decisions, to what extent did you involve others in your thinking? How open-minded were you towards others' views or ideas? As an excellent leader, you do not have the monopoly on all the good ideas or all of the answers.

The picture below is a fairly well-known one. Take a look at the picture for a moment and describe what you see...

You should be able to make out an image of a woman. But is the woman you see a young woman or an old woman? If you show this picture to a number of people some will see an image of a young woman and some an image of an old woman. If you can only see one image and have trouble seeing the other, ask someone else to point out the main features of the other.

Whether you have seen this image before or not, the important message is that the picture has *both* images but your brain chooses to see and fixates on just the one image.

Don't forget

You may have come up with some excellent ideas in the past but others probably also have some great ideas if you just bother to ask.

As a leader, you may be able to come up with some perfectly valid solutions but it's always worth considering that there could also be many other solutions that you are just unable to see.

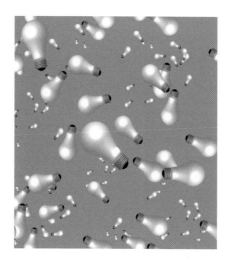

You can therefore benefit greatly from involving others to ensure you get a greater breadth of ideas or viewpoints.

Sounding board
In the same way that you want to encourage others to use you as a sounding board to test out their ideas, so you should be able to use others as your sounding board and this can only help to further develop a climate of trust.

Not decision-making by committee
When talking about valuing or seeking alternative views we are not suggesting that decisions should be made by committee. As we will explore further in Chapter 8, this is rarely an effective or efficient way of making decisions.

So ultimately, as leader, you will be faced with making decisions and with determining which ideas are best taken forward. It is far better that this is done from a position of strength having considered a range of options.

Beware

Asking for different opinions and views is not about abdicating responsibility for making the final decision.

Supporting behaviors
Excellent leaders who appreciate the value of considering others' viewpoints are likely to do so based on strengths in the following behaviors:

- *Interpersonal Awareness* – People demonstrating this behavior will empathise with others and therefore be able to see things or at least appreciate things from others' viewpoints

- *Conceptual Thinking* – This behavior is about being able to relate possible disconnected ideas as well as having a general breadth of thinking

Welcoming Views

Asking for and welcoming others' views and ideas sends out a strong message about the type of leader you are and the relationship you want to have with those that work with you.

Keep people informed

It's very important to keep people informed over how their ideas or views are used and, where appropriate, that you give credit to others for their specific contribution. By doing this they and others will be encouraged that their ideas are being listened to and actioned. As a result they are more likely to provide further input in the future.

Killing off input

A word of caution: This is not a ploy to merely *look* as if you're listening to others' views in order to persuade them you're involving them in decisions when, in reality, you have no intention of listening to alternative views. Doing this will ultimately backfire and lead to a significant breakdown in trust.

Here are some other sure fire ways to kill off people's willingness to offer ideas and suggestions:

- Hijack others' ideas and take the credit for them yourself

- Ask for ideas but then dismiss them or criticize them immediately

- Welcome ideas when they are given to you but then do nothing with them or forget to feedback progress

 Beware

It is so easy to break down the climate of trust and discourage people from wanting to contribute their ideas.

So, having looked at how to successfully kill off people's enthusiasm for offering suggestions and ideas, let's look at the more positive aspect of how best to elicit views from others. As we explored in Chapter 1, much of this is about developing a positive and trusting climate so that people feel their views matter and are being listened to.

Make it natural

Encouraging people to put forward their ideas is not just about using contrived mechanisms such as 'suggestion boxes'. These may have their place on occasions but their benefits are often short-lived and best used when linked to a specific need or project.

We are really talking about creating an underlying climate that encourages people to feel they want to contribute to discussions and express their views as part of everyday interactions, within meetings, as well as within specific ideas-generating workshops.

Break down the barriers

New ideas are not the sole domain of senior management. Encourage even your most junior staff to come up with ideas and to express their views. Some of the best ideas and opinions may come from those who are closer to the work itself or whose views are not cluttered and colored by years of past experience.

Encourage the obvious

Some people, especially when new, can feel self-conscious about asking 'stupid questions'. Quite often, however, these turn out not to be the stupid questions, just the ones that others have thought of asking but have not been brave enough to ask.

Hot tip

Don't just think of generating ideas as a one-off activity. Look at how you can encourage people to make suggestions at any time.

79

Valuing Others' Differences

From our exercise on Page 76 you will hopefully appreciate that others can often see or comprehend things differently to you. Looking back to where we explored personality traits and behaviors in Chapter 2 should also provide enough evidence that we do not all think the same way. We know, for instance that some individuals are more focussed on detail whilst others tend to think in 'big pictures'.

Value difference

If you are not someone who naturally attends to detail, it is particularly valuable to ensure you make a special effort to consider the views from those who do have such attention. Your tendency may be to think of such individuals as hindering or unhelpful but often nothing could be further from the truth.

Ask an introverted personality type to describe an extrovert and they will tend to describe the extrovert using negative terms such as 'loud', 'shallow-thinking' or, perhaps 'loves the sound of their own voice'. Ask an extrovert the same question and they will naturally respond with positives such as 'expressive', 'quick-thinker' or perhaps 'gregarious'.

The same applies the other way round. Extroverts cannot easily appreciate the positive side of being an introvert whereas introverts naturally can. I have posed these questions to many groups of individuals categorized earlier by this one trait and invariably get the same responses.

These differences go well beyond just introversion and extraversion which is why it is so important to respect others' perspectives.

Hot tip

Whether you are an extravert or an introvert, look for the positives in the other – remember there are positive attributes to both traits.

Thinking styles

As well as considering individuals' different personalities and behavioral strengths it is worth noting here that people also process their thoughts and imagine things in quite different ways. For instance, when asked to imagine an event or situation from the past, some people will literally see images of the event – perhaps even playing it out as in a movie. Others are more likely to imagine the situation based predominantly on the sounds they conjure up. A further group will tend to think of the situation based on how they feel and the sense of touch.

These different styles of thinking are important to recognize and we'll be looking at this fascinating area in more detail when looking at visualization techniques in Chapter 7.

Team dynamics

Whether building a team from scratch for a specific project or working with your existing team, it is likely that it will consist of individuals with a range of different skills, experiences and personality types.

It is important to try to understand and even profile the strengths and styles of those within the team so that you can ensure you work to bring out each of their strengths to achieve the desired outcome. Encourage each member to contribute their different perspectives over the task in hand based on the role they are being asked to perform.

Hot tip

Even if you have worked with a team for a while it can be very insightful to profile each member to determine their personalities and thinking styles.

Diversity is Good

There are so many ways in which we are different from each other. As a leader, these differences are to be celebrated, valued and, most importantly, embraced. We are not talking here about doing this just because it's what the Law states – which, of course it does. Nor from any sense of trying to unite the world, however laudable this may be. As a leader you should celebrate diversity from the very hard-nosed fact that this can significantly improve the effectiveness of your decision-making and generation of ideas.

Defining diversity

Looking at a broad definition of diversity, the more obvious categories include:

- Race
- Gender
- Ethnicity
- Age

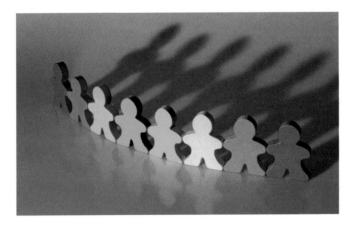

Each of these groupings brings with it different perspectives on life, work issues and situations. But beyond the above recognized diversity groupings there will also be big differences in viewpoints based other perspectives such as an individual's:

- Geographical and environmental background
- Family and social background
- Educational or political status

Beware

Don't just deal with issues of diversity from a legalistic point of view. There are real benefits in recognizing and working with individuals' differing viewpoints.

Keeping an Open Mind

It is very easy to get into the mindset of looking for all the downsides in arguments and ideas – after all, as leaders, we are expected to question and check before making informed decisions. However, as we have already discussed at length, this can be quite unhelpful and ultimately damaging.

Here is a simple technique you can use to stop yourself from focussing on just the negatives:

1 Welcome the idea – this can be as simple as saying thank you for raising the point

2 Come up with at least one aspect you like about it. This forces you to think about the idea from a positive point of view – after all, the individual must have thought it was a good idea to have raised it

3 If necessary, say you'll give it some further thought and get back to them. Of course, make sure you do!

Step 2 is clearly the most important one. Sometimes it can be useful to actually state out loud what you like about an idea. If you do need to put forward a view, try to add to the idea rather than merely criticize it: "One thing which I'll add to build further on this idea is..."

It's about empathy
The important point is that it forces you to empathise with the individual who has raised the idea and this in turn helps you to think outside of your normal mindset.

Even if you are just reading material, if you hear yourself thinking of all the downsides of what you are reading, force yourself to think of at least one positive aspect as well.

Hot tip

When considering another person's idea, try to think about the positive aspects which would have prompted them to raise it.

Generating Ideas

You and your team may, from time to time, need to generate new ideas. If the issue is relatively straightforward it may be possible to think through the issue and simply come up with a few ideas on your own.

Where the issue is more complex or you are looking to generate more creative solutions, the subject may benefit from having a number of creative minds focussed on it. It may still be possible to merely ask others their ideas or opinions but there may also be occasions when a more dynamic approach could provide more interesting and creative results. The simplest way to generate ideas within a group is through brainstorming.

Brainstorming

Most people have come across or participated in a brainstorming session and will appreciate therefore that it can be a very quick and effective way of generating many ideas or of gaining a number of different perspectives on an issue.

Sadly, many brainstorming sessions ignore the simple rules that are essential if you're to get the most out of the session. Here are some of the most important rules...

Hot tip

Brainstorming can be a very effective way of generating new ideas or comments provided, as facilitator, you follow these simple rules.

Keeping up the momentum

The best brainstorming sessions are ones that are very energetic and fun. Keeping the energy levels high and ensuring everyone is participating can sometimes be a challenge. Here are some simple tips to help keep everyone engaged:

- Start with a warm up exercise that's fun and preferably not work-related

- If possible, get everyone standing up rather than just sitting in their seats or at desks

- Don't leave the scribing to one person – let people write their own comments so that everyone feels more involved and the writing process is speeded up

- Give 'Post-its' to individuals or pairs and get participants to write their ideas on these to stick on a wall or board

- It can sometimes help to move 'Post-its' into themes so that people can start to see patterns emerging – involve others in developing the themes with you

- Keep asking for more ideas and constantly phrase the question or problem in different ways

- Look out for and encourage quieter individuals who may have great ideas but are just not so vocal

Keep pushing

Initial contributions tend to be the more obvious responses whereas the later ones are often more obscure and interesting. So don't stop when there is a lull in activity. This is the point to get people thinking harder – you'll sometimes be rewarded by some real gems when you push people in this way.

Hot tip

Don't just stick to the same format for brainstorming. Try different exercises and techniques in order to bring about variety.

85

Thinking And Creativity

We have already spoken about the need, as an excellent leader, to value diversity and to consider individuals' different perspectives regarding issues. This is especially the case when considering brainstorming and creative thinking.

Draw out the quieter ones

Remember that some people are naturally more introverted in terms of their personality traits and will not necessarily be outspoken in their views. This does not mean they don't have any ideas. In fact their ideas, when they do express them, are likely to be more carefully thought through and therefore definitely worth listening to. When asking others for ideas, be aware of the personalities involved and try to ensure you draw out comments from everyone.

Adaptive or innovative?

Based on individuals' thinking styles and personality traits you will discover that some individuals are very capable of *innovating*, that is, being able to develop new ideas and concepts from a 'blank sheet of paper', dealing with big concepts and radical change. Others, however, are far more comfortable *adapting* existing ideas and concepts or making changes on an incremental basis.

Much work has been done to understand these psychological differences between people's ability to handle and instigate change – we have directed you to resources to find out more, in Chapter 10. It is important at this stage to at least be conscious of these differences in terms of your own level of creativity and those in your team. This is especially important when taking people through change and is something we will cover in Chapter 7.

Don't forget

Introverts tend to do more thinking than talking and so may not be the noisiest but could have the most valuable contributions to make.

Supporting traits and behaviors

In terms of traits, innovative thinkers will generally be more *Carefree* and *Open*. In terms of behaviors, they are more likely to be strong at *Conceptual Thinking* and possibly also at *Strategic Thinking*.

Adaptive people, on the other hand, are more likely to be *Closed* and *Conscientious* in terms of their traits. They are also likely to be stronger in behaviors such as *Analytical Thinking* and *Attention to Detail*.

Remember that your behaviors, and especially your traits, are enduring aspects of your personality and therefore relatively difficult to change significantly. It will be far easier to work with your existing strengths than try to change your overall thinking patterns and behaviors.

Don't forget

Behaviors and traits are not that easy to change. Work within your personality profile and use others' strengths to support you.

More creative exercises

There may be occasions when you find that your creative juices just aren't flowing. This can be especially the case when the subject is one you've explored many times before or when there is a need for you to generate solutions that are particularly creative or original.

In these situations your thinking is likely to follow well-trodden thought patterns. The challenge is therefore to find ways to break through your old style of thinking and to look at the problem from different perspectives.

There are many interesting and challenging exercises you can use to help you and your team generate original solutions in this way. In Chapter 10 you will find some useful resources to help you.

Summary

- There are often many more solutions or perspectives on an issue, although you may only be able to see one option. Open your mind to the possibility that others may see things differently to you

- You can still seek others' views even if, ultimately, it's you that needs to make the final decision

- Just as you can act as a sounding board for others, work to develop a climate where others can be your sounding board

- It is no good just asking for ideas unless you back this up by actioning them and letting others have feedback on how their ideas have been used

- Encouraging others' ideas is not just about having a suggestion box. It's about developing a climate where people feel able to express their views and ideas at any time

- People think in different ways and will therefore approach issues in very different ways. Utilize these differences to ensure you uncover all aspects of an issue

- Diversity should be welcomed to add richness to ideas and discussions. Different cultural, social and educational backgrounds can bring very different views on an issue

- Value and work with differences in viewpoints when building and working with teams

- Ensure you maintain a positive mindset towards ideas rather than always looking for problems or the downsides

- Brainstorming can be an effective way to quickly gain new ideas and comments from people but make sure you stick to the simple rules to ensure it is run effectively

- Be aware that some people are better at coming up with fresh new ideas whereas others are more suited to adapting existing models and ideas

- It's important to encourage those who are naturally quieter or have a more introvert profile to share their views. Often these views can be drowned out by those with louder voices

5 Maximizing Performance

A key role of any leader is to maximize the performance of those working under their direction. Most people will thrive and grow when they feel engaged and motivated in their roles. This chapter considers the many elements of performance management that an effective leader needs to consider.

About Motivation

Motivating people is a complex subject to explain. It's an even more complex issue to put into practice. What motivates one person can be a complete turn-off for another. Many managers believe they can engage and motivate others based on what motivates *them* but unfortunately this is rarely an effective tactic.

Back to childhood

To understand what motivates people we need to go back to the subject of personality and behaviors. In particular, we need to consider childhood experiences and the activities that gave us the greatest pleasure during that period in life.

Try to remember back to when you were around six or seven years old. When you had the freedom to choose, what were your favorite games or activities? Let's consider three different childhood experiences:

Hot tip

The games and activities that gave you the greatest pleasure as a child are likely to give the best clues to your underlying motivational profile.

- **Construction kid** – This child especially enjoys playing by themselves, building the biggest and most elaborate constructions from kits or building blocks.

  They enjoy the challenge and intricacy of the task in hand and the concentration that's needed. Of course, they also get pleasure from seeing the end result of their labors.

- **Team player** – This child likes playing games with other children. They probably enjoy playing board games or, if more active, playing team games with other children outdoors. They get a buzz from being with others and from the social interaction that comes with these activities.

- **Team captain** – This child is similar to the team-player but this child also likes to decide what games are played, the rules of engagement and is also, on the same basis, likely to be the one to pick the players for his or her team.

You may be wondering how this links to motivation and leadership. The fact is that the types of activities we enjoyed most as a child give a big clue as to the types of activity that are still likely to motivate us most today.

Your motivators today

If you were a 'construction kid' and enjoyed tasks that involved accuracy; attention to detail; focussing on completing a project; you will have praticed these behaviors more and will tend to therefore still enjoy them in a business setting and perhaps have become good at them at the same time.

Similarly, if you enjoyed being a 'team player' and, in particular, the social interaction and feeling of team achievement, you will, in all probability, still thrive on interactions with others in the work environment.

Bringing forward the behaviors of being a 'team captain' to the work environment, if you were a child with this motivation profile you will most likely be motivated today by being able to set the direction; by choosing those to work in your team. You will probably gain satisfaction from seeing others grow and succeed following your involvement.

Motivators differ

By seeing these simple linkages between the activities enjoyed during childhood and the related work-based motivators, you can hopefully see that people are motivated and driven by very different factors and activities.

Your job, as leader, is to identify and understand (not guess) what motivates those in your team and specifically key into these motivations in order to energize and get the very best from them.

Beware

Don't assume that others will be motivated by the same things as you. Make sure you take time to find out what motivates someone.

More on Motivation

If we take the three childhood themes a stage further we can draw these out into three simple scales of motivation – these were originally developed by the psychologist Henry Murray:

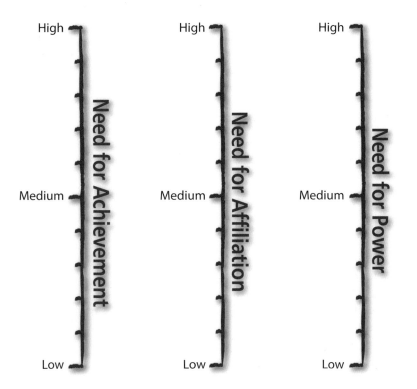

Motivation scale definitions

Here are more specific definitions for each of the three scales:

- **Need for achievement** – a desire to accomplish tasks, master skills or achieve targets or goals. People with a high need for achievement like to be recognized for their success and will strive to have goals they can then accomplish.

- **Need for affiliation** – a desire to be accepted as part of a social group. It can also be a need to be liked or loved by others. People with a high need for affiliation won't want to do things that may result in them not being accepted or liked.

- **Need for power** – a desire to see things happen as a result of personal influence. People with a high need for power like to put themselves in positions of control or social influence. They like to get things done through others.

Hot tip

Take some time over deciding your profile – even a few weeks if needed. You need to dig below what you are forced to do in your job to what really drives you.

Assess yourself

After thinking about these definitions, place a cross on each of the three scales to indicate your relative levels of motivation. Bear in mind these are relative scales and so you are unlikely to be high on all three scales, however motivated you are! Use your childhood experiences to help inform your profile. Ask yourself what really gives you the greatest satisfaction at work, not because you *have* to do it but because you *enjoy* it.

Motivation and competence

Just because you're motivated towards an activity does not necessarily mean you will be good at it. There is, however, a greater possibility, that if an activity interests you, you'll do it more often and therefore, through practice, become good at it.

Managing motivations

Motivations rarely change and therefore role changes can lead to interesting challenges from a motivational perspective. Take, for example, a top sales person who is asked to take on a coaching or mentoring role for a new salesperson. If the new mentor has a high motivation towards the *Need for Achievement* (which may have been their driver as a salesperson) they are likely to be more motivated to sell themselves to achieve personal targets. They may get little satisfaction from watching someone else develop.

Don't forget

An individual's motivational profile changes very little and therefore a change of role will not affect their underlying motivation – this could affect how well they adapt to a new role or activity.

It's not to say that this person shouldn't be given such a role but they may need to find alternative ways to motivate themselves based on their underlying motivational profile. In this situation it may be helpful to set the mentor targets (to give them a personal achievement) based on how they will develop the sales person. Their motivation can therefore still be satisfied based on achieving a result and, importantly, the new sales person still gets developed!

Performance Management

Performance management is a term often mistakenly used to describe an appraisal process. But true performance management is so much more than just a once or twice yearly meeting to discuss an individual's progress.

Assuming a positive climate

Assuming you have built a positive climate based on elements such as trust, empowerment and clarity of role, you will probably find that most of the management of an individual's performance will be picked up by the individual themselves. They are likely to want to take responsibility for setting and monitoring their own standards of performance by:

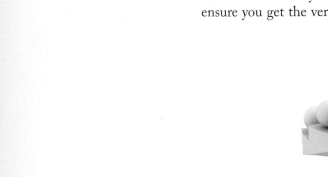

Don't forget

If you have developed a positive climate in the first place, much of the work of managing performance will be picked up by individuals themselves.

- Determining or agreeing overall personal objectives/goals

- Setting milestones or sub-goals

- Defining what success will look like

- Setting appropriate timescales for goals and sub-goals

- Highlighting any development needs in relation to the completion of the above objectives

Where do you fit in?

So, it would seem that provided you have created the right climate such that people take personal responsibility for their own goals, there's nothing left for you to do. Clearly this is not the case. There are still many ways for you, as leader, to add value and so ensure you get the very best out of people.

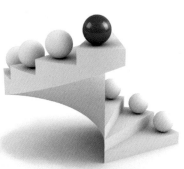

However well-motivated an individual is, there are always ways in which you can help to enhance an individual's performance. You can, for example:

- Ensure the individual's objectives are totally aligned to the overall vision and organizational objectives

- Help the individual to focus by asking questions – this is something we will look at shortly

- Ensure there is an appropriate element of 'stretch' within the individual's goals

Too ambitious

Paradoxically, in order to get the very best performance from someone, you may sometimes need to be the one to pull them back. This would be the case where you believe the individual is being too ambitious over their goals. If an individual over stretches themselves they run the risk of either becoming dispirited and therefore giving up or, alternatively, they may just try to take on too much and end up not achieving any of their goals.

Clarity

Another important way in which you can add value to an empowered individual is to help them be clear about what it is they want to achieve. An individual may, for example, state that they want to set themselves an objective: *'To increase their accuracy levels relating to the entry of client data.'* By asking probing questions you can help them determine:

- What increase in accuracy they need to achieve?

- What, specific client data this relates to?

- What impact this accuracy will have on meeting deadlines?

- How will they measure their new effectiveness?

Beware

Don't encourage people to be over-ambitious. There is a chance they could fail and this could have a negative impact on their confidence.

Setting Clear Objectives

There are many goal-setting models being used, the most common are based on the acronyms 'SMART' or MARC'. Here's what these generally stand for:

Hot tip

Whichever goal-setting model you use, it's just as important that the goal is motivational – we'll cover this later in this chapter.

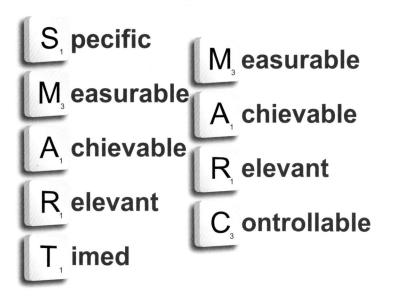

It's about clarity

The purpose of using either of these models, or any other of the many variations out there, is to ensure that there is clarity and a common understanding over the goal being agreed. At the point when a leader and an individual agree an objective there should be no misunderstanding over what has been agreed.

There is nothing more demotivating than for an individual to have energetically pursued a goal only to discover that this was not was originally expected by the manager.

Making it motivational

These goal-setting models are probably the most commonly used by managers and, certainly in terms of providing clarity and conciseness, they work. But it's quite possible to set goals based on one of these models and yet to miss the most important element of any goal – to be motivational or energizing.

Being a leader, rather than just a manager, requires you to agree clear goals but also ones that leave the individual feeling totally energized, committed and confident they can achieve them.

The whole purpose of a goal is to leave the individual feeling they can and will achieve what is needed in the agreed time-frame.

Personal responsibility for setting objectives

As with all other elements of leadership, it's far more empowering for an individual to set, or at least have a significant input to, their objectives. If the individual is sufficiently engaged, the objectives set by the individual are likely to be at least as challenging as any you would have set.

More importantly, when an objective has come from the individual themselves, they are far more likely to want to achieve it than if it is one imposed by you or where there has been little or no input from them.

Questions to ask

Based on the 'SMART' model, here are some example questions which you can ask in order the help add the missing element of motivation to the goal-setting process:

- **Specific**

  Describe to me the detail of what it will look like when you complete this objective

- **Measurable**

  How will you know when you have achieved this objective?

  What simple measures can you set in place for you can keep a track of your progress?

- **Achievable**
  On a scale of 1-10 how confident are you that you can achieve this goal?

- **Relevant**
  How do you see this complementing or supporting your other work activities?

- **Timed**
  What is a realistic timescale to achieve this based on your workload and the needs of this piece of work?

Hot tip

Using a 1-10 scale can help with putting a measure on and discussing something which is difficult to tangibly quantify.

Making Goals Challenging

Goals should normally incorporate an element of challenge in order to stretch the individual and so get the very best out of them. However, as we have already suggested, people tend to react differently to goals based on their underlying motivational profile and their personality. As a result, setting a very challenging goal for one person might help to spur them on to higher levels of performance whereas for another they may feel overwhelmed and so completely turned off by the prospect.

Challenge needs to be personalized

The level of stretch or challenge within a goal therefore needs to be personalized to the individual. As we have stressed many times, the best way to personalize objectives is to ask the individual. You simply need to ask: 'How stretching or challenging do you feel this objective is for you?' Sometimes it can help to ask how challenging the objective is on a 1-10 scale.

Ask them

If the individual responds that it is only a low challenge – say 3 or 4 – then you can legitimately ask: 'How can we make it more interesting and challenging for you?'

It's important not to either assume they will be challenged by what would challenge you or to guess what you think would be more challenging. Instead, simply ask them.

Hot tip

If they say a goal is not very motivational take time to explore this and understand how you can make it more motivating.

Low challenge

You may think that on occasions it may be more helpful to incorporate either no challenge or a low challenge within the objective just so that the task is easily attainable and gets done. Unfortunately, this often have the opposite effect.

When an objective is set with too low a level of challenge, some individuals – often linked to their motivational profile – will decide to make the task more interesting by adding their own (potentially distracting) challenge, resulting in the original objective not being achieved.

Beware

Setting a goal with no or little challenge is just as likely to not be achieved as a challenging one.

Jumping exercise

This simple exercise is one I sometimes use on development courses as an icebreaker:

Provide each participant with a small sticky label and stand them next to a clear wall with a relatively high ceiling. Instruct them to jump as high as they can and to place the sticker on the wall as high as they possibly can.

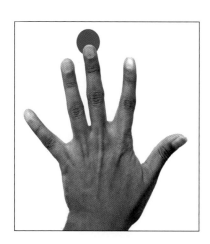

Now repeat the exercise with a second sticker and invariably you will find that individuals are able to beat their first attempt. This means that on their first attempt, however willing they were, they did not achieve to their full potential. You may find they improve again if given a third or even a fourth attempt.

Contributing factors

So what could lead to this improvement without any additional input? The most important factor is that on the first attempt individuals are faced with a blank wall and so have no idea of their capability. On the second jump they have their first sticker to aim for and most will see this as a benchmark to beat. In other words, they can see what they have already achieved and this gives them more confidence for their second jump. Of course it is also important to note that it is *their* first sticker they're aiming for and not one that *you* have put on the wall as *your* target.

Making Goals Manageable

Whilst it's normally beneficial to agree or set goals with a degree of challenge it is also important to be mindful not to set goals or objectives that are too challenging. If a goal appears unattainable you run the risk of the individual giving up or not even trying for fear of failure. This is represented by the 'A' in our two goal setting models on Page 96 which stands for 'Attainable'.

That is not to say that you should avoid large or ambitious goals but, where you do have large or ambitious goals, you may need to look at ways of making them appear more manageable.

Break it down

One of the simplest ways of making a goal more manageable is to break it down into smaller, more palatable sized sub-goals.

Before you do this, though, take a step back and let the individual or team decide whether it feels too big. What appears over-ambitious or off-putting to you may feel perfectly attainable to them. Assuming they do feel the goal needs breaking down into smaller sub-goals, ask them to define the size of the sub-goals rather than define them yourself.

One step at a time

There are two benefits of encouraging an individual to define their own sub-goals. Firstly they will develop a stronger sense of ownership over the process and their goals. Equally, though, you will encourage the individual to think logically about the milestones within the project that will ultimately define success.

Hot tip

Getting the individual to work out their sub-goals helps them to break down the objective and so understand the overall goal better.

Sub-goals not tasks

It's important when encouraging an individual to break down a goal that they focus on determining sub-goals that each contribute towards achieving the overall goal as opposed to simply describing tasks or actions.

Sub-goals, like full goals, describe a point of achievement rather than the pursuance of an activity.

Of course, once an individual has defined their sub-goals they will then want to determine how best to achieve these. But defining tasks too early encourages an individual to think in too much detail about completing the tasks instead of focussing on what success will look like.

Looking back

Another way in which you can make a goal feel more manageable, especially where the individual expresses a lack of confidence, is to encourage them to recall a large or complex goal they previously completed successfully and to think how they tackled it last time.

Positive visioning

It's all too easy to fall into the trap of allowing an individual to start bringing in negative thinking whereby they start to convince themselves that they can't complete a task or objective. This mindset, where the individual convinces themselves they are going to fail and so puts little effort into trying to achieve the goal, can so easily become a self-fulfilling prophesy.

As you discuss a new objective with an individual it's of critical importance, therefore, that you encourage them to immediately vision a positive scenario in which they successfully complete their objective rather than a negative scenario.

Beware

It's critical to talk about sub-goals not tasks. If the individual talks about *doing* something instead of *achieving* something, they are not talking about goals.

Strengthening Goals

Using either SMART or MARC as mnemonics to remind you of the key elements of an effective goal is fine. But in reality, this only goes a small way towards setting in place an enduring and energizing goal.

Following a meeting to agree an objective, so much can happen to get in the way of even the most empowered and motivated individual. Barriers or obstacles could include:

Hot tip

Ask the individual to determine up front what barriers they envisage could occur to prevent the successful completion of the objective.

- Other work commitments

- Resistance from colleagues

- Interruptions such as holidays or illness

- Emotional or personal problems at home

- A lack of confidence that they really can do it

Predicting potential obstacles

Whilst some eventualities can't be easily predicted, it is surprising how many can. By exploring all the possible barriers or obstacles at the time the objective is being agreed you can encourage the individual to determine up front a number of possible mitigating measures for each one.

If the individual is subsequently confronted by one of their identified obstacles, they won't be immediately thrown off course because they will already have thought through some potential solutions to help deal with them should they arise.

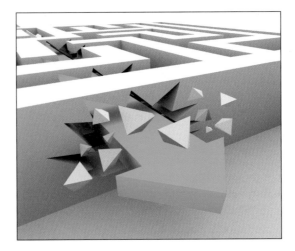

Visualizing the end goal

Encourage an individual to bring their end goal to life by asking them to visualize and describe to you what it will be like when they have successfully achieved their goal.

Not only will this motivate the individual but it may also help them to define and describe a successful outcome and so be able to recognise it when they do achieve it.

Questions to ask

Here are some questions to help you focus them on what a successful outcome would be like:

? What will the successful completion of this objective look like/feel like/be like for you?

? On a scale of 1-10 how important is achieving this goal to you. What does that score represent to you?

? How will you recognize when you have successfully achieved this objective?

Make it colorful

The more realistically and vividly the individual can visualize the objective the more motivated they are likely to be towards the objective and more clearly they will be able to align the activities to achieve the objective.

It's important that this visualization comes from the individual and not from you. However clearly you are able to describe an outcome, it will not be their vision and so will not have the same motivational impact.

Hot tip

The more realistic and vivid you can encourage the individual to be when describing their end goal, the more motivational it is likely to be.

Reviewing Objectives

Unless the objective is a relatively quick and straightforward one, it's advisable to review progress well before the objective is due for completion. Reviewing at the end can only result in it either being considered completed or not. If it hasn't been achieved, it may be too late to do anything about it. It's for this reason that annual – or even six-monthly – appraisals are generally not frequent enough for effective performance management.

Try to encourage interim reviews so that any issues can be identified as early as possible and any remedial actions set in place. These may be linked to regular one-to-one meetings with individuals or diarized specifically for the purpose.

Beware

Don't leave the review of an objective right to the end. By then it may be too late if there are any performance issues.

Their responsibility

If the individual has been fully involved in the initial setting of the objectives and totally empowered and engaged in what they are being asked to do, you should find that they are keen to take the lead and feed back their progress – probably without you even having to prompt them.

Involving you

If at any time an individual feels they are falling behind with their objective they should be able to bring this to your attention without feeling they are going to be unduly criticized. Instead, they should feel they can seek your advice or reassurance over their chosen method of delivery.

Self-criticism

Ask most individuals how they feel they are performing and more often than not they will be overly critical of their own performance

Where this happens, this leaves you, as leader, the task of putting any performance issues into perspective and then focussing on the positives. Where their criticisms are in your view realistic, focus their attention on what will help to bring them back on track.

Hot tip

People are likely to be far harder on themselves than you could possibly be. This normally leaves you the more positive role of balancing the review with the good aspects.

104

When Things Don't Happen

So far in this chapter we have concentrated on the positive side to objective setting where the individual or team meets their objectives. But this may not always be the case. There is the possibility, for a number of reasons, that the objective is not met. This could be because:

- They didn't understand what was required of them

- They had other conflicting priorities

- They didn't have the necessary skills or knowledge to accomplish the objective

- They lost motivation for completing the objective

- Other dependencies out of their control stopped or hindered their progress

Can't do vs. won't do

When an objective has not been met, one issue to determine is whether the reason the individual didn't achieve their objective is because they *couldn't* do it or whether they could do it but *wouldn't* do it. If it is a matter of capability then your approach can focus on ensuring that next time they do feel capable – either through training or ensuring any possible blockages to them achieving the objective are negated.

If, on the other hand, it was because they wouldn't do it, your approach is likely to be very different. In this situation you will need to uncover the underlying reasons why they didn't feel motivated enough to complete their task which, in your view, they were otherwise quite capable of completing.

Beware

It is important to determine whether any performance issues are as a result of poor motivation or attitudinal issues as no amount of training is likely to solve these.

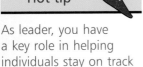

Maintaining Focus

An important function of a leader is to help individuals and teams stay on track and totally focussed on the things that matter. However capable and motivated people are, there are reasons why they could lose focus. For example:

- They are so deeply involved in the task in hand that they lose sight of the bigger picture. In other words they can 'no longer see the wood for the trees'

- They are faced with a number of competing priorities all appearing to be of equal importance

- Where a task or project is long-lasting they may start to lose sight of the original goal

- If they are over-enthusiastic, they may try to take on more than they can realistically handle

This is a good reason why, as leader, you should avoid getting embroiled in too much of the detailed delivery. It then puts you in a far better position to see things from the outside and therefore maintain overall focus.

Bringing them back on track

Your role in these situations is to help an individual re-focus. In most situations the most effective way of doing this is to ask the individual questions so that they get the priorities clear in their minds. You may just need to simply ask them how their current activities support the overall objective.

In terms of priorities, get them to take step back and re-evaluate what's important and then encourage them to keep focussed on just one or two key priorities.

Questions to ask

Most importantly, in order to achieve a significant objective or goal, individuals may have defined a number of sub-goals. In attempting to achieve these sub-goals, there is a risk that they will lose sight of the original overriding goal.

Depending on the circumstances, here are some example questions to ask to help maintain an individual's focus:

? Can you describe to me the end goal that we originally agreed. What will overall success look like?

? How relevant is what you are doing to the overall objectives?

? Are there any of the things you are doing now that don't directly contribute to the end objective?

? What could you realistically drop so that you can focus more closely on the most important priorities

? On a 1-10 scale, how focussed are you right now? How could you improve your overall level of focus?

Problem areas

We are, of course, assuming that the individual is fully committed to the objective and there are no other performance issues such as them choosing to pursue their own agenda or just picking the fun or easy tasks at the expense of the things that really need doing. Where you suspect this to be the case you may have to spend time discussing their motivations to bring them back on track.

Beware

A lack of focus may be just a personal organizational issue or it could be something more fundamental related to a lack of motivation towards the objective.

107

Recognizing Top Performers

However empowered an individual or team, the one thing that needs to come from you, as leader, is recognition for excellent performance.

Focus on the positive

Too often managers focus on the negatives and forget to look out for the positive elements of performance. In fact, sometimes the mindset of some managers is that good performance is what employees are paid to do and therefore to be expected. Yet recognition, just through simply noting and praising someone's efforts can have a very positive motivational impact on an individual or team.

Of course, the most obvious time to recognize and praise excellent performance is at the successful conclusion of a piece of work. However, especially when a piece of work spans over a long period of time, this may not be sufficient.

Actively look out for opportunities to recognize excellence or special effort such as:

- When an individual masters a new skill or activity

- When someone volunteers to take on a new responsibility

- When you first see a small improvement

- When you get feedback from others on an individual's performance

- When someone reaches a particular milestone or sub-goal

Don't over-do it

Whilst you should always be looking for opportunities to praise, make sure it is deserved, in proportion and genuine. Over-doing the praise can devalue its effect and so become meaningless.

Appropriate recognition

Just saying well done in person directly to the individual or team may be sufficient – even an email to say you've noted what they have done can have the desired positive effect.

Be careful praising someone in front of others. It can have a positive effect on the individual and also demonstrate to others how you appreciate and recognize good performance. However, depending on the individual, it may be embarrassing for the recipient or even divisive if others don't often get praise.

Rewarding good performance doesn't need to involve a material reward – although that may be appropriate on occasions. Recognizing excellent performance could include:

- Giving the individual additional responsibilities

- Allowing the individual to take on a special project

- Putting the individual on an enhanced development or 'fast-track' programme

- Featuring the individual in the organization's employee magazine or intranet

Praise immediately

It's important to be responsive when recognizing good performance. Don't leave it a long time before you say or do something. A quick spontaneous act is likely to be far more appreciated than something more involved that only happens weeks afterwards.

Hot tip

Try to think of new ways to acknowledge good performance so that the recognition is noticed and appreciated.

Summary

- Our motivations are deep-seated, probably originating from childhood. What motivated us then, can provide clues to what motivates us today

- Don't assume that what motivates you will motivate others. Motivation is a very personal thing so rather than tell them, ensure you ask what will help to motivate the individual

- If the individual is fully engaged they will want to play an active role in setting their own goals and objectives

- Use a goal-setting model such as SMART to ensure that goals are clearly understood by all parties involved

- It's important to ensure objectives incorporate an element of stretch or challenge but not so much that the individual is discouraged from trying

- If goals are especially big or complex it can help to break them down into more manageable 'chunks' so that the individual is not put off by the scale of the challenge

- Setting goals without giving consideration to potential barriers could leave the individual exposed to the possibility of hitting a problem and not knowing how to handle it

- Try getting the individual to visualize the outcome. This can help to bring a sense of reality to the objective and help to motivate the individual

- The review of the progress of objectives is best when it comes from the individual themselves especially as they are likely to be more critical of their performance than you

- When reviewing performance, if there are problems it's important to distinguish between *can't do* and *won't do*

- An important role of an effective leader is ensuring the individual or team remains focussed on the most important activities

- Recognizing and rewarding good performance is an important and often forgotten role of a leader. Look for opportunities to recognize good performance

6 Developing Talent

One of the most critical roles of a leader is recognizing the capabilities of those working for them. Developing individuals so that they grow to become the leaders of the future can be extremely rewarding.

Developing Others

One of the most rewarding elements of the role of leader is helping others to develop and grow in their roles. Development is so much more than just putting people on training courses – in fact, most personal development happens in the normal working environment and not in a classroom environment.

Development should be thought of from two different perspectives:

1   Developing people to meet the needs of the business and to deal with specified capability gaps

2   Developing people to support their career development and their long and short term career aspirations

Of course, on occasions these two needs may be met by the same development activity but, more likely, they will be two quite different agendas.

You may have quite a good idea of what is required in terms of development to meet the needs of the business but when it comes to helping someone develop as part of their personal career aspirations, you will need to spend time exploring their ambitions – without adding your own agenda or assumptions.

The development paradox

I have heard many managers state that they deliberately avoid asking their employees about their career aspirations for fear that they will say that their next move is going to be outside of the organization. Worse still, they have avoided developing people for fear of developing them to the point where they are more marketable elsewhere. This attitude is shameful but also based on a wrong assumption. The paradox is that more often than not, the more you invest in someone's development and more marketable you make them, the more they tend to want to stay.

Don't forget

Investing in people's development is more likely to encourage people to stay with an organization.

Choosing what to develop

You will want to ensure that any development activity is focussed and targeted at delivering a specific outcome. So requests from employees such as: "I've been on a project management basic level course, so can I now go on the intermediate level course?" should be refocussed on what, specifically, they need to develop and how this intermediate level course is expected to deliver that.

Defining the gap

Whether the focus is on a defined business need or based on an individual's personal development need the first step is to define the difference between where they are now and where they need to be – this is often referred to as the 'development gap'.

 Beware

Don't succumb to requests for training and development without properly analyzing the real need.

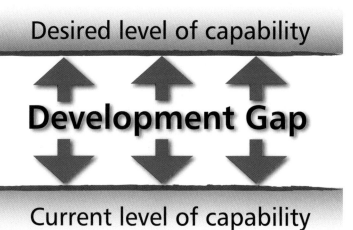

113

Probe for detail

When getting the individual to define their current level of capability spend time really probing the individual – not simply to find faults but to help the individual fully understand their needs.

Confidentiality

If any real value is to be gained from such a discussion, it is essential that the individual feels totally at ease about opening up and describing honestly their current capability – both the positives and the negatives. This requires particular sensitivity and presumes a level of trust has already been developed. This is something we explored in Chapter 1.

Development Options

So, development is far more than just putting someone on a training course. Of course this may be one option but even then, unless the course is tailored to the individual's need and framed with other development activities to support the overall learning, the full benefit of this type of intervention is likely to be wasted.

Tailored solutions

The suitability of different development options depends on:

- The nature of the development needing to be addressed

- The learning style of the individual themselves

- The resources (including budget and time) available

The development need

Development needs can range from very simple, easily learned needs such as a new piece of knowledge; more practical skills which may take more practice and experience in order to perfect through to highly complex and deep-seated behavioral issues such as those described in Chapter 2.

Knowledge-based needs may be addressed by simply reading appropriate written material or through conducting online research. Practical skills may initially require the learning of some underpinning knowledge before then acquiring and practising the skill itself.

Behaviors on the other hand, being so deep-seated, may need long-term development solutions such as coaching to gradually understand and then learn new patterns of behavior.

Some suggestions

On pages 176-7 we have suggested a range of development solutions split into those useful to develop knowledge-based needs and those to develop skills-based needs.

Hot tip

There are very many more ways of developing someone than putting them on a training course. Explore the possibilities with the individual.

Learning styles

We all have our preferred way of learning – our learning style. Some people prefer to sit with a book and learn from what they read, for others this would leave them cold.

Some prefer to 'jump in at the deep-end' and just give it a try whereas others couldn't contemplate putting themselves to the test without having completely learned and perfected the required skill first. Some need to see a practical example of what is being asked of them and yet others like to question and test what is put before them.

Given that your learning style is likely to be different from that of the individual you are discussing development activities with, your best bet (as we discussed relating to motivation in the last chapter) is to ask rather than assume. Find out what methods of learning suits the individual and jointly explore what solutions may be most suitable for the development need being addressed.

Resources

Budget is one of a number of resource issues to take into account when determining the most suitable development solutions. It may not be realistic or necessary to put one individual through a costly training programme especially if the budget also needs to stretch to cover others.

Time away from normal work is another important factor to consider. The ideal solution may be achieved through simple work-based activities without having to take someone away from their work for days at a time.

Sending someone on a bespoke training solution may also conflict with established organization's processes if the individual is taught different and possibly conflicting models and systems.

115

 Beware

Don't try to recommend training based on your preferred learning style. Activities need to suit the individual, not you.

Coaching For Performance

Coaching can be a very effective way of developing an individual and when conducted by the individual's line manager can help to strengthen the bond and understanding between both parties.

Coaching defined

Coaching is an ongoing development discussion whereby the coachee (the recipient of the coaching) is encouraged to take personal responsibility for their development through focussed questioning by the coach.

In the business context the focus for coaching will normally be on issues relating to maximizing the coachee's performance in their role or on helping the individual to work towards achieving their career aspirations. For this reason coaching is often regarded as an integral part of a leader's role.

Coaching can be performed by someone other than the individual's direct line manager – perhaps a respected work colleague or other manager – but, generally, the benefits of the manager performing the role of coach make it the best option.

Ongoing relationship

The critical element of coaching is that it is ongoing rather than just a single intervention. As such,. it can be of particular benefit for dealing with longer-term issues such as behaviors or more complex skills. Meeting and reviewing progress every few weeks gives the coach and coachee the opportunity to agree incremental, highly focussed, development activities.

Between coaching sessions, the coachee will be expected to pursue the agreed development actions that will help them towards the completion of a development sub-goal. In a sense, these sub-goals are similar to organizational sub-goals discussed in the last chapter – it is just that the overall goal is related to the individual's personal development rather than a business goal.

Hot tip

Only consider coaching once you have built up a good level of trust with the individual.

Goal setting rules apply

All the same principles we outlined in the last chapter for organizational goals apply when agreeing development goals and sub-goals. They should be SMART or MARC; they should be stretching but achievable; above all, they should be motivational, especially as they relate to the individual's personal development.

Coaching process

The general process for a coaching session can follow a similar format each time as described below. Most importantly, throughout the meeting the coach should *ask* the coachee rather than tell or advise:

Beware

Watch you don't take responsibility by advising and telling. Instead, ask the coachee so that the responsibility is left with them.

1. The individual discusses and describes their long-term goals in relation to the issue being developed

2. This long-term goal or 'aspiration' is broken down into smaller, more manageable sub-goals where necessary

3. The most appropriate sub-goal is chosen and becomes the prime focus of the coaching discussion

4. The current capability relating to the chosen sub-goal is explored to define the development gap – see Page 113

5. The individual is encouraged to decide (based on their learning style) the best actions to address their sub-goal

6. After exploring any barriers to them completing the actions the individual pursues their agreed actions

When the coach and coachee meet again to review progress they may concentrate further on the chosen sub-goal or, if achieved, move onto the next sub-goal, picking up the process from Step 3.

More help

The above process as we have described here is a very brief outline of a typical coaching meeting. If you are interested in exploring coaching further then the author has also written a book in this series entitled: '*Business Coaching in easy steps*'

Identifying Top Performers

As part of your succession planning process you will no doubt want to look out for your very best performers – those with the ambition, drive and potential – to develop and progress further in the organization.

It would not be realistic or practical to expect every employee to develop into a key role within the organization but you may wish to identify at least a small number who you want to invest in by providing more focussed development.

Identifying Potential

Spotting individuals who are highly motivated and who are effective in their current role is relatively straightforward. They will probably stand out from the rest based on their performance figures, achievement of their objectives or just from their overall positive demeanor. Identifying individuals who you believe have the potential to develop into leaders of the future or key specialists in their field, however, is a far more complex and tricky business.

Behavioral profiling

An individual's behavioral profile – bearing in mind that this is likely to be relatively stable – can provide a good indication of an individual's potential to develop into a top role. Assessing someone's behavioral profile can be achieved through a behavioral or competency-based interview and feedback.

If you have received training in behavioral interviewing, this may be something you can conduct yourself, otherwise you may need to ask a trained interviewer to conduct this on your behalf. The independence of another person conducting such an interview can be helpful anyway.

Don't forget

You are not just looking for good performers in their current roles but for people who have the potential to develop further.

Personality profiling

Another useful way of profiling individuals in order to assess future potential is to use one of the many forms of psychometric assessment or personality tests available.

Either used independently or in conjunction with a behavioral interview a personality assessment with feedback conducted by an experienced person can be a very useful way of assessing the potential of individuals.

The feedback itself, as well as being helpful in assessing the profile of an individual, can be used as the basis for an initial development discussion.

Assessment centres

A very thorough form of assessment involves developing a battery of different tests, assessments and simulation exercises. These can be used to assess a number of potential candidates at the same time but need to be carefully structured and planned.

Fair assessment

It is critical that whichever process you choose to assess potential and to highlight possible future high performers is fair. It should be conducted in such a way that all individuals being assessed are treated equally based on a set of pre-defined criteria. Offering the opportunity to be assessed to just a few favoured individuals could be seen as divisive and demotivating by those not picked.

What about the rest?

Of course, following an assessment process, if some need to be told they are not suitable for further development, this too can be highly dispiriting. For this reason, any process that you plan to use to identify top performers needs to be very carefully and sensitively thought through.

Hot tip

Don't abandon those not chosen for career development. At least feedback the outcomes of any assessment and use this data to highlight particular development needs.

Developing Future Talent

Once you've identified one or more individuals who you believe can be your future leaders and talent you then need to invest time and effort into encouraging, supporting and developing them.

There are many options open to you in order to develop your potential stars and they are not mutually exclusive. Options to consider include:

- Creating a tailored development plan

- Providing coaching specifically focussed on their career needs

- Offering them the option to be supported by a mentor

- Putting them through a formalized leadership programme

- Funding an MBA or other Masters level course

- Providing psychometric assessment and feedback if not already conducted as part of the assessment process

- Fast-tracking their career with enhanced opportunities

- Providing special project work to provide enhanced exposure

As with all development options, the choice of activities will, to a large extent depend on the learning style of the individual concerned. Whatever options you consider they should, again, be applied fairly to all those involved in the process.

Formal vs. informal

Formal learning such as an MBA program can be very thorough and beneficial for the right individual. It will also result in a formal recognized qualification.

It can be a costly option, however, both in terms of money and time away from the ongoing work commitments. It could also be duplicating a lot of material that the individual already knows.

Hot tip

Before committing to expensive formal development programmes, discuss with the individuals how best they learn and the needs they have

Coaching

As their manager, you may already be holding regular coaching sessions relating to issues of performance with individuals in your team. Applying coaching to the subject of career development can be a very focussed way of providing support and developing your most talented individuals.

You may be able to combine coaching sessions with regular performance coaching sessions or agree to meet completely independently when discussing issues relating to their career development.

Mentoring

An alternative to coaching is mentoring. As we shall explore shortly, mentoring sessions may follow a similar process to coaching but often involve a more senior manager in the organization who can provide an independent perspective to an individual's development quite different from the performance-related coaching provided by their immediate manager.

Hot tip

The kudos and increased exposure gained from offering someone a mentor can be highly motivating.

121

Having the roles

Whatever development you choose to provide to support your most talented individuals, they must feel that there is benefit in investing their time and effort in the development process. There is no point in energizing and motivating individuals, building them up to be the future of your organization, if no roles are likely to be available for them in the foreseeable future.

Mentoring vs. Coaching

There is often confusion over the meaning of the terms 'coaching' and 'mentoring'. To a certain degree this is an issue of semantics and you will find that in some organizations these terms have become interchangeable.

It is, however, worth making a distinction between the two. We have already defined coaching as being an ongoing relationship and this is normally also the case for mentoring.

One difference is that the main focus for mentoring is usually on the longer-term career aspirations of an individual. Another important difference is that the mentor is usually a more senior influential player in the organization rather than the individual's line manager.

Lighter touch

A mentoring relationship is likely to be a lighter touch than is the case with a coaching relationship. Coaching discussions tend to concentrate on performance related issues and, as such, will tend to require review meetings every few weeks. As mentoring relationships tend to focus on longer-term career aspirations the meetings between mentor and mentee may occur less frequently – perhaps only every month or even less frequently.

Influence

One of the benefits of using a mentor who is a senior figure within the organization is that they can play an important role in providing influence. The mentor may, for example, be able to create opportunities for the mentee to get exposure at meetings or events that might not normally be made available to them.

A more senior manager may also be in a position to persuade others in the organization, or others from outside, to provide valuable experiences that will help build the mentee's profile.

Hot tip

If possible, give the individual a choice of mentors so that they can pick someone they know they will have confidence in and trust.

Same process

The coaching process we outlined on Page 117 can also be used by a mentor when discussing career aspirations with a mentee. Using such a process helps to add structure to a mentoring relationship which can otherwise tend to turn into an informal chat and therefore lack real benefit.

Other roles of a mentor

In addition to the more structured review of specific career issues, a mentor can play other useful roles in support of the mentee. For example by:

- Acting as a sounding board over particular career options

- Providing alternative viewpoints over issues (providing these are not structured to conflict with the individual's manager)

- Providing an additional pair of eyes when looking out for good performance for the purposes of recognition

Mentor and coach

The individual's mentor is likely to be a different person to their line manager. It's important, therefore, that the mentor and line manager work together to ensure that their activities complement each other and do not duplicate or conflict with each other.

Confidentiality

That said, as with any development relationship, it is critical that any discussions held between the mentor and mentee are kept strictly confidential. The mentee must have confidence to be able to open up their true thoughts and provide an honest appraisal of their capabilities without the fear of any discussions being fed back to their line manager without their prior consent.

Any discussions between the mentor and the individual's line manager will need to be kept at a high level to avoid disclosing sensitive detail.

Don't forget

It's important that the individual feels comfortable to open up about their development needs. This will only happen if they know their discussions will be kept confidential.

Being a Mentor

Having described the role of a mentor, it's worth exploring what it means to be a mentor and how best to perform the role from a leadership perspective. Being asked to be a mentor for someone is a great opportunity to use some of the experience you have gained throughout your own career for the benefit of others.

It is an additional responsibility that may not have any direct benefit to your day-to-day work but should be regarded as a longer-term investment in someone's career development and perhaps part of the organization's overall succession planning programme to develop its future leaders.

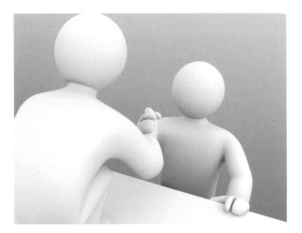

Benefits of being a mentor

As well as the benefits to the mentee, there are also benefits to being a mentor. For instance:

● The opportunity to take stock of and perhaps share some of your own career experience

● A reinvigoration of your own role by taking on this additional responsibility

● The opportunity to gain perspectives from a more junior employee about how it feels to work in the organization

● A refreshment of your own leadership style based on the, perhaps, more youthful perspective of a newer manager

● An opportunity for the cross-fertilization of ideas between different departments

Don't forget

Whilst the focus of the development is on the mentee there are great benefits for the mentor in performing the role.

Getting to know you

Don't force yourself upon your mentee. Suggest you meet for an initial introductory meeting so they can work out whether they feel comfortable with you and trust you as their mentor. If, at the end of that meeting, they are not sure then you may want to offer to find an alternative to act as their mentor.

Non-directive

When mentoring it's especially important that you do not direct or lead your mentee. You may be tempted, especially if you are more senior, to think that your role as mentor is to tell and advise your mentee so that they can benefit from your many years of experience and wisdom. This, however, puts the focus on the past and may possibly result in you trying to teach your mentee old-fashioned ways of doing things instead of thinking for themselves.

Encourage through questioning

As with any other form of leadership, you can encourage your mentee to take personal responsibility by asking probing questions rather than telling. It is far more motivational and forward-looking to question, challenge and encourage your mentee to think through issues for themselves.

Example questions

Clearly, your questions will depend on the subject being discussed and the circumstances involved but, as an indication, here are some examples of the type of questions you could ask:

? What's important to you at the moment regarding your life and your career?

? How would you describe this as a career goal?

? What made you choose that particular career path?

? How committed are you to this career choice – say, on a scale of 1-10?

Hot tip

Don't force yourself upon a potential mentee. Arrange an introductory meeting and start by exploring some possible ground rules.

125

Evaluating Development

As with all aspects of business activity, it is important to put in place appropriate measures to evaluate the effectiveness of any development activity.

Appropriate measures

We say 'appropriate' because, whilst it is important to put in place measures, they should not be so onerous that the job of evaluating takes up more time and effort than the activity itself.

Wherever possible, measures should be put in place that are readily available or form a natural part of a business process.

Defined from the goal

During your early discussions with the individual you will have most likely explored their development goals and possibly sub-goals.

If you have encouraged the individual through questioning to describe what it will be like when they achieve their development goal or objective, this description will give some important clues to what needs measuring.

Different levels

Classic training theory suggests that you should be looking to evaluate the effectiveness of training and development at four different levels:

 Was the training appropriate? That is, if they went on a training course, was it enjoyable, stimulating and covering useful content? For classroom training sessions this can be measured by getting delegates to complete end of course feedback forms or 'happy sheets'. With more informal training it may be as simple as asking the individual whether they found the development activity useful and interesting.

Beware

Evaluation is important but don't let it get in the way of the development activity. Keep it simple.

2 **Did the learner learn what was expected of them?** This can be measured through the use of short tests or skills assessments immediately following the development activity to see whether the development activity has resulted in the individual learning to the required level.

3 **Has the development changed the way the learner does things in the workplace?** However good the development activity, it's only really worth doing if, as a result, the individual starts doing things differently. This is one of the most important measures as it demonstrates that the development activity has transferred into the workplace environment.

Hot tip

Sometimes performance drops before it improves – especially when developing a new skill.

4 **What difference has the development had on the bottom line performance of the organization?** This is the ultimate test of the effectiveness of a development activity. It is, however, often difficult to prove that any organizational improvements have been as a direct result of an individuals' development. Sometimes there may be a significant lag following the development activity before organizational performance is impacted and can be measured.

Don't forget

Ultimately most development should improve bottom line performance but bear in mind there may be a lag before behavioral improvements filter through to this level.

Responsibility for evaluation

As with all leadership activity, it is best for the responsibility for the evaluation of development to be left with the individual themselves. They will have a clear idea from your initial discussions about what they need to achieve and what success will look like. Your focus for evaluation can be more around level 4 relating to overall organizational impact.

Summary

- When looking to set in place development for those in your team, ensure that it is focussed on specific needs such as clearly defined performance or career development needs

- Spend time defining the development gap – that is, the difference between the individual's current level of capability and where they want or need to be

- The choice of development activity depends on the type of development need and also on the individual's learning style

- Coaching is based on an ongoing development relationship and therefore lends itself towards longer-term development needs including behavioral development

- Coaching relies heavily on goal-setting and so the same goal-setting principles still apply

- It is important that the emphasis for coaching is on encouraging the individual to think through issues for themselves rather than the coach 'telling'

- Identifying future talent for development is about identifying potential rather than just current performance

- Whatever methods you use to identify individuals with talent you should apply them fairly so that those not chosen are not left demotivated

- Developing future talent can be achieved through formal learning and development or through more informal development such as coaching or mentoring

- Mentoring is similar to coaching but usually the mentor is a more senior figure in the organization and the focus is on the individual's longer-term career needs

- Being asked to be a mentor can be very rewarding – there is as much to learn from being a mentor as being the mentee

- Evaluation of training and development needs to be considered at four different levels - from whether the development intervention was rewarding through to bottom line organizational performance

7 Leadership in Practice

We have so far focussed on many of the underlying principles behind being an effective leader. In this chapter we build on these by examining some of the practical elements of leadership.

Thinking Strategically

Strategy or plan

These days the term 'strategy' is used far too often in business conversation when referring to anything from a training strategy through to an investment strategy. It's not to say that it's not possible to think strategically about these sorts of topics but, more often than not, what people are really referring to is a training *plan* or an investment *plan*. Even the game of chess is referred to by many as a game of strategy – in reality it is a game of tactics.

Strategic behaviors

It may help to refer back to the behavioral descriptions in Chapter 2. To think strategically you will clearly utilize the behavior *Strategic Thinking*. You may also use other behaviors such as *Conceptual Thinking* and *Client Oriented Thinking*.

The essence of thinking strategically is that you need to pull yourself away from dealing with detail to think about more fundamental long-term issues and potential outcomes.

Taking time out

Many of the activities of a leader can revolve around dealing with day-to-day business delivery – supporting, delegating, developing and motivating people. When in this mode of thinking it can be very difficult to get into a truly strategic mindset. It is advisable therefore to set aside specific time, perhaps each week, to focus your mind on thinking strategically. Teams often arrange 'away days' to consider strategy just to extract people from their normal environment and patterns of thinking.

It's not always about 'blue sky'

Whilst we are referring here to high level and potentially long-term issues, when considering strategy, we are not necessarily referring to 'blue sky' thinking This is a term which often refers to the generation of fresh new thinking and ideas. Of course these may form a part of your thinking but it is just as likely that your strategy will be based on existing products, services and organizational positioning.

SWOT and PEST

Thinking strategically means thinking beyond the 'here and now' of your organizational activities. It's critical to be aware of the capability of the organization itself but also to understand the environment or space in which it operates. For this purpose it can be helpful to conduct a SWOT analysis and also a PEST analysis. More details of these well-known exercises can be found in Chapter 10.

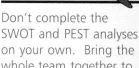

Hot tip

Don't complete the SWOT and PEST analyses on your own. Bring the whole team together to ensure you get a breadth of perspectives.

Strategic questions

Here are just a handful of questions that will help to ensure you are thinking strategically:

? What is the true purpose of the organization/team?

? How do we compare with the competition and how can we therefore differentiate ourselves from the rest?

? In what ways can the team/ organization build or sustain a competitive advantage?

? What are our core strengths and are we fully utilizing them?

? What is distracting us from delivering to our strengths?

Visioning The Future

We explored goal-setting on Page 103 and how visioning can strengthen the process by helping to bring a goal to life. Visioning is a technique you can also use when exploring the future and especially when needing to engage others in your future vision.

Describing your vision

Whatever your vision, try to make it as clear and vivid as you can. Immerse yourself totally in your future vision – it can help to do this at a time when you are not likely to be interrupted.

To make it as realistic as possible, try to build a vision that involves all of your senses:

- What do you see? – Imagine looking around you and take in your surroundings. Who is with you and what is happening around you? How do you see the organization performing in the future?

- What do you hear? – Imagine people talking. What are they saying and how do they sound? Hear what your customers are saying or, perhaps even your competitors

- What do you feel? – When thinking about your future scenario, what mood are you in and how are others around you feeling and responding? If appropriate, think about how your clients are feeling.

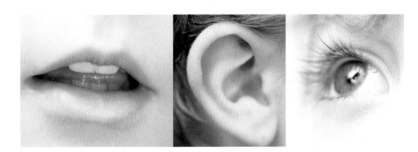

 Don't forget

Visioning does not always mean imagining pictures - it is best when it involves all of the senses.

We have used the term 'visioning' when referring to the act of thinking about and describing the future, yet you will realize that we tend to use more senses than just sight. Some people naturally think about scenarios using pictures and visional triggers, others tend to 'vision' based on other senses such as hearing, feeling and even smell – these are known as 'thinking styles'.

Adapt your language

Because of the differences in people's visioning styles it's important, when sharing your vision with others, to describe it using a combination of senses. Phrases such as: "I can see this organization growing..." or "Looking into the future..." are clearly prompting visual thinking and will therefore appeal more to people who naturally think using pictures and visual cues.

Phases such as: "This sounds like a great way forward" or "I can hear them applauding this one even now..." will appear to those with a dominant auditory thinking style. On the other hand, people who base their thinking on touch and feeling – what is referred to as *kinesthetic* – will be more attuned to phrases such as: "I feel this one is going to be a great success.." or "If we grasp this opportunity we can...".

Bring people with you

It is highly frustrating to have witnessed some of the most visionary leaders failing just because they have not been able to translate their vision effectively and express it in terms that are fully understood by others.

In behavioral terms, this is about employing behaviors such as *Adaptive Behavior* and *Persuading/ Influencing*. Think carefully about the audience you are trying to engage and the best language to get your message across.

Beware

If you have a dominant thinking style you may be tempted to only describe your vision using this sense. Try to engage people by describing your vision based on others' styles.

133

Positive and vivid language

Ensure that you think and express your vision in positive terms both to yourself and to others. As well as appealing to the different senses, try to use language and descriptions that are bright, clear and emotionally engaging. As with all elements of leadership, be enthusiastic but, above all, genuine.

Turning Visions Into Reality

Having a clear vision is important. Engaging others in that vision, as we have just described, is also critical. But the most important element of all is turning your vision into a workable solution that delivers the required outcome.

Supporting behaviors

Looking back at Chapter 2 you will see that behaviors likely to support the transformation of a vision into reality include those within the *Delivering Results* cluster of behaviors.

Creating a business or project plan will benefit from behaviors such as *Analytical Thinking* and *Attention to Detail*. Seeing that plan through to completion will benefit from *Tenacity, Concern for Excellence* and, possibly, *Client Oriented Thinking*.

Different profile

You should notice that these behaviors are very different to those supporting the creation of an organizational vision and strategy and, as such, you may find you are not strong in both sets of behaviors.

Where you recognize these deficiencies, ensure you engage others around you who can work with you to develop the detail within your plans. This will not only ensure that the detailed elements of the plan are developed effectively but it will also involve those that are likely to be responsible for the delivery at an early stage and so help to gain their full commitment.

Don't forget

Having a great vision is only half the story. You then need to turn your vision into tangible outcomes.

Working to a plan

Even for relatively small pieces of work it is normally useful to work to a plan. Working things out as you go along is not only unstructured and ineffective, it also makes the job of involving others far more difficult.

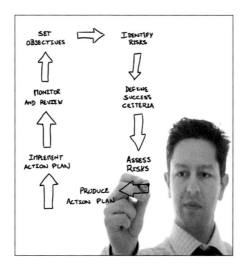

At least committing a project to a documented plan provides a platform for discussion. Outcomes can be clearly expressed, roles agreed and, most importantly, milestones and measures put in place.

Staying on track

With appropriate measures defined, keeping on track can be a relatively light touch activity for the leader. Provided measures or key performance indicators are met, you may not need to have an active role other than to receive regular progress updates. Those trusted with the responsibility for the project will know at what point you need to be alerted to problems or, hopefully, success.

Seeing it through to completion

Many leaders are good 'starters' but not all can truly lay claim to being good 'starter-finishers'. In terms of a leader's role, seeing work through to completion does not necessarily mean doing it all yourself or even being responsible for the interim monitoring.

It does mean ensuring all the pieces of the plan are in place that will ensure work is driven through effectively to deliver the desired outcomes. It also means being tenacious over more difficult stages of a project in order to overcome difficulties and so ensure success.

Influencing others

One area in which you, as leader, can play an active role is in influencing key stakeholders in order to ensure particular projects receive appropriate levels of support. This is where the behavior *Stakeholder Relationships* can be very useful.

Hot tip

Being a leader who is concerned about measuring outputs does not mean having to do it all yourself. Others in your team, if suitably empowered, can still be responsible for measuring its effectiveness.

135

Inspiring Others

What makes an inspirational leader? Why is it that some leaders just seem to naturally inspire others and so attract and develop great teams and individuals around them? In reality, it is not down to a single attribute or personality trait – it can be a combination of factors including:

- Demonstrating high levels of personal energy and enthusiasm

- Being a trusted leader with high levels of integrity

- Having a proven successful track record

- Having a positive but realistic approach to work

- Demonstrating genuine empathy and belief in others

- Having confidence in (but realistic about) their capabilities without being big-headed or ego-centric

Being an inspirational leader does not mean having to be loud, or extravert or having to make impressive and emotional speeches. It is quite possible to inspire others whilst at the same time being quietly spoken or more introvert by nature. Above all, people are inspired by leaders who are genuine, and true to themselves.

Behavior breeds behavior

People will naturally emulate the behaviors of those they are interacting with. If you, as leader, demonstrate energy and enthusiasm, this will inevitably rub off on those around you. If on the other hand you are negative or unenthusiastic it is difficult to expect others to act any other way.

Take a critical look at the way you come across to others and think about how they respond to you as a result.

Hot tip

Be constantly aware of your energy levels and levels of enthusiasm. Others will quickly pick up on any changes in your mood and react based on this.

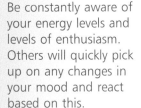

Welcoming Change

It's time to stop introducing every new project and presentation with the words 'We live in changing times...'. It is a worn out cliché and, in reality, this is the way life and business have been for very many years and is how it is likely to continue in the future. For many, especially the younger generations, they've never known it any other way.

Standing still is not an option

For the vast majority of working environments, this is the way that businesses maintain a competitive advantage. To stand still is not an option as this would mean going backwards in real terms. The same applies to individuals' development. Even those that want to stay in the same or similar roles need to continue to learn and develop just to keep up with the pace of change.

Encourage change

Whilst there's no call for making changes for change's sake, encourage a climate where people not only embrace change as a natural part of their working life but actively seek out and suggest opportunities for improvements. These may be incremental improvements or more radical ideas for wholesale change.

Challenge 'sacred cows'

Sometimes organizations develop 'sacred cows' – rules or processes that have been in place for so long, nobody is prepared to question or challenge their continued existence. Don't let 'sacred cows' develop and, where they already exist, encourage people to identify them and challenge their current validity.

Leading Through Change

However positive the change and the climate in which it takes place, there will always be individuals who find the process more difficult to handle or take on board. There may be a number of reasons for this:

- Certain roles may be negatively impacted by the proposed change – even lost entirely

- Individuals may be expected to take on additional responsibilities which, whilst positive overall, may leave them feeling unsure of their capabilities

- There may be misunderstandings over what changes are being proposed

- There may be differences of opinion over what the best solution is for the proposed change

Beware

However positively you describe and justify a proposed change, there is always the possibility that some will react negatively to the proposal.

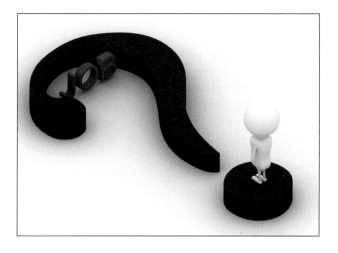

Sensitivity needed

Whilst all of the above situations are quite different, the one leadership quality which is called for is sensitivity. Clearly, where there is a potential for roles to be lost this needs to be handled with great care and in line with appropriate employment legislation. Initially, however, it may not be clear which roles are to be lost. For this reason many more employees may feel under pressure than are ultimately affected.

Even when it's clear which roles are impacted, those remaining may continue to feel threatened and lacking in confidence.

Reassurance

If individuals need to be retrained or are being asked to pick up additional responsibilities they may initially feel reticent or even threatened over the prospect of failing. Once it is clear what their new roles or responsibilities are, arrange time with each individual to discuss their concerns and to explore any development needs they may have relating to their new activities and to reassure them that you believe in their capability to perform the new role.

As we described on Page 113, you will also need to explore any development gaps – that is, the difference between their current capability and the capability requirements for their new role.

Stakeholder analysis

Misunderstandings over proposed changes can be significantly reduced by setting in place effective communications throughout the change process. Prior to the commencement of any change, consider all of the affected parties or stakeholders and determine their stance over the proposed changes.

Agree how you are going to engage these individuals, ahead of the change where necessary, in order to gain their support or active involvement. This is where the behavior, *Stakeholder Relationships* becomes particularly useful.

Strong Leadership

However perfectly you plan and deliver change, there is always the possibility that some individuals will disagree with the proposed changes. This may be as a result of the impact on their roles or because they disagree with the chosen plan. This is where, as a leader, you will need to demonstrate firm yet sensitive leadership. Provided you believe your decisions have been taken after full consideration – something we will be considering in the next chapter – then you should have the confidence to see through your changes.

Hot tip

'Survivors' of change may still feel concern and anxiousness. Make sure you spend time on a one-to-one basis understanding their concerns.

139

Building a Team

Whether you are considering a team to deliver your normal business activities or creating a team specifically to deliver a finite project, you will want to have the very best combination of people working with you.

Of course where you inherit an existing team, you may not initially be in a position to make many significant changes to its composition. It may be possible, however, to make changes over a period of time as new individuals are brought into the team. It is therefore still worth getting to understand the profile and dynamics of your existing team so that any future team changes can be made in a coherent and logical way.

Profiling your team

The ideal profile for your team will very much depend upon the nature of the work needing to be undertaken. Once you are clear what work needs to be undertaken it is worth considering what the ideal make up for your team needs to be. Ask yourself:

- Does the team have the right levels of competence in terms of knowledge and skills or will you need to provide training and development in areas where there appear to be skills or knowledge shortages?

- Does the team have the most appropriate behavioral profile to support the required work? Are there any essential behaviors that your team doesn't have – if so, you may need to consider bringing in individuals with the required supporting behaviors unless you have the time to develop them.

- Does the team have sufficient diversity? Where a range of viewpoints is useful to the work, you may need to consider whether your team has sufficient diversity and breadth of experience to provide an appropriate mix of ideas.

Getting the team to bond

You may have a good feel for the profile of your team but initially this may not be understood or appreciated by those in the team. Whilst you are not expecting team members to become life-long buddies, they do need to understand their relative strengths and respect their fellow team members for what they contribute to the whole project or piece of work.

Team-building exercise

Most people think of team-building exercises as ones involving demanding challenges such as abseiling down cliff tops, solving specially devised business conundrums or other such engineered events. These do have their place, especially when used to break down hierarchical barriers or to build trust and confidence amongst team members.

However, for many situations, a simple workshop is sufficient if designed in such a way that it helps to share the various strengths and personality profiles of team members.

Myers-Briggs Type Indicator (MBTI)

Whilst they can have their limitations, profiling tools such as Myers-Briggs Type Indicator or MBTI can be used quite effectively in some team building situations.

Rather than worrying about the precise details of each individual's profile, the best way to utilize such tools is to use the overall data to inform a professionally facilitated team workshop, where individuals are encouraged to gain a better appreciation of the different personalities and capabilities of those in their team.

Hot tip

MBTI is just one type of profiling tool. Take a look in Chapter 10 at the range of resources available to you and your team.

Cross-Functional Teams

Leading a cross-functional project team brings with it a certain set of challenges especially where, as leader, you do not have any line authority over those working in your team. You may even be leading a team including your peers or individuals who are more senior than you.

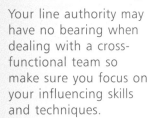
It's about influence

Much of the skill in leading such teams is in the way you inspire and influence those in the team without the need to exert your direct authority. In reality, this is very much how any team should be led. It is far more effective to engender a climate of cooperation and respect with your team members than to try to force your leadership on them.

Wide-ranging disciplines

Quite often cross-functional teams are brought together to tackle issues that have a wide-ranging impact on an organization. As such, they may need to pull together representatives from a number of disparate functions and specialisms.

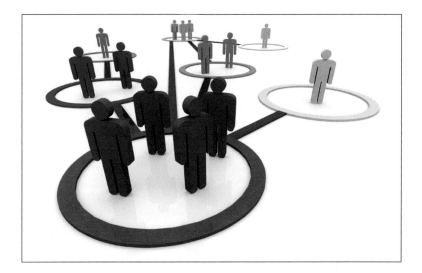

In these situations, you cannot be expected to have a detailed working knowledge of all these disciplines. Your role, as leader, is to provide the over-arching vision and direction so that everyone is working towards a common set of goals. You are also there to facilitate effective communication between the various functions to ensure that all interests are taken into account.

Common language

Individual disciplines bring with them their own distinctive sets of jargon and language. Try to discourage jargon and acronyms to ensure there is clarity and understanding across all the representative functions. Set or agree goals that are clearly understood by all parties and from time to time check to ensure that everyone understands what is being asked of them.

Other work

When leading cross-functional teams it's often the case that your team members will only be 'on loan' to the project from their function and normal daily work. This means having to be especially mindful of their other day-to-day work commitments.

Be realistic about the amount of time you can reasonably expect from individuals, especially if people appear to be over-committing themselves to your project. This additional activity may appear very interesting and engaging but the individual's line manager may not be so impressed if this is at the expense of their normal work.

Supporting behaviors

The behaviors that support the leadership of a cross-functional team are very similar to those needed for a general leadership role. In particular, however, it is useful to be able to call on behaviors from the *Relationships* cluster such as *Stakeholder Relationships*, *Influencing/Persuading*, and *Interpersonal Awareness*.

Hot tip

Acronyms can get in the way of effective communication. Keep it light-hearted by encouraging the team to point out unnecessary use of jargon and TLAs (three letter acronyms!).

143

Don't forget

Respect the fact that those in your team may only be doing this work in between their normal work responsibilities.

Summary

- Thinking strategically is far easier when you have the opportunity to take yourself away from the day-to-day detail of work

- Visioning isn't just about visual imagery – it also helps to involve all the sensory cues to build a truly vivid vision as well as to engage people who naturally use other senses to those you use

- Having a vision is fine but it is also critical that a leader can develop a plan to deliver that vision and see it through to completion

- If you are not naturally a 'starter-finisher' then make sure you have someone in your team who will ensure your work gets seen through to completion

- Be inspiring as a leader by having personal energy and enthusiasm for your work. Ultimately it will rub off on those around you

- Welcome change and encourage those in your team to constantly look for opportunities for change, however small

- Change can impact people in many different ways. At the start of a change project, map out all those who are likely to be impacted and determine how, from the outset, you will deal with these people

- Sometimes even those who are impacted positively by change need reassurance and additional training in order to build their confidence over their new responsibilities

- Building a bonded, energized and well-suited team with all the right skills and behavioral qualities is difficult. Take time to profile what you really need from your team first

- At the start of a project it can help to bring the team together in a way that they can find out about each other's strengths. This can be as simple as an introductory workshop

- Leading a project consisting of cross-functional members can be challenging – you may need to work hard at your influencing skills

8 Decision Making

As a leader you need to be able to make decisions that are effective and timely. Not only is this essential in terms of the decision itself but also it helps to build confidence with those in your team.

Gathering All The Facts

Decision-making in business is rarely a simple matter of choosing between two options. The options themselves may be highly complex, numerous and often with outcomes that are far from certain. Even the issue itself may not present itself in an obvious way and may need considerable investigation to truly understand all the interrelated issues.

Time critical

Effective leaders tend to avoid jumping to immediate decisions based on a 'gut-reaction' or instinct. Having said that, often time is a critical factor and procrastinating over making a decision or spending an unrealistic amount of time gathering every last piece of available data may, in itself, negatively impact on the ultimate outcome. We will look at making decisions by instinct later.

Beware

Don't procrastinate or take too long gathering data to support your decisions as this may have a negative impact on the outcome

146

Data gathering

Try to establish right from the start what information you'll need in order to fully understand the issue and to make a decision. In broad terms the sort of factors you may want to consider are:

- What is the problem or issue I'm trying to solve?

- How long do I have to make this decision?

- How easy it is going to be to find this information?

- Who else's perspective on this issue would be useful?

- What are the consequences and risks of making the wrong decision?

Seeking the right information

Setting off on a 'fishing expedition' in search of any related information can be highly unproductive. Not only will it inevitably use up unnecessary time and resources, it is also likely to bury you in so much irrelevant data that you may miss some of the critical information you really need to see.

So consider carefully, right from the start, what data will truly put yourself in the position of being able to make an informed decision.

Soft and hard data

When gathering facts to support your decision or idea, you will most likely initially think about gathering the hard facts relating to the issue. Hard facts may include performance data; client responses; financial information indicators; statistical or market information.

In addition, though, make sure that you also think about the 'soft' or qualitative information that can support your decision making.

Soft data is more difficult to measure than hard data – it includes information such as client attitudes; how employees are likely to react to the decision; possible media attention or perhaps even the reaction of the financial markets.

Supporting behaviors

A useful behavior supporting the gathering of information is *Analytical Thinking* and this is often accompanied by the behavior *Attention to Detail*. Understanding the breadth and complexity of the issue may also be supported by *Conceptual Thinking*. Of course, where the issue relates to a customer issue, it may also help to have a behavioral profile strong in *Client-oriented Thinking*.

Hot tip

Be choosy about the data you collect - too much can swamp you and bury the important information.

147

Synthesizing The Information

Problem analysis

The best way to start, perhaps even prior to gathering your information, is to write a short, highly focussed statement of what the problem is that you are trying to solve or make a decision over. Without this clarity it is quite possible to find yourself solving the wrong problem – that is, solving a different issue based on assumptions or incomplete information.

Try to distill your problem definition down to just one or two statements. Your definition should not describe the cause of the problem – we will look at this next – nor should it describe solutions. Just state the situation and, where applicable, its impact.

Root cause analysis

Where the issue being considered is complex, it may be necessary to drill down into the detail of what is at the root of the problem or issue. There are a number of analysis tools available to help get to the root cause of an issue including 'fishbone' or cause and effect analyses. However, one of the simplest methods is to keep asking 'why?' – just as small children do. For example:

- Clients are complaining that response times for answering their queries are too slow... WHY?

- Because our call centre operators are having to pass technical queries to specialist teams... WHY?

- Because the call centre operators are not trained to deal with complex issues... WHY?

- Because the call centre was originally formed based on a different operating model and we still recruit unskilled call centre operators... WHY?

This process of questioning can continue until you can no longer ask 'why?' – at that point you should have your root cause.

Looking for trends

Once you've gathered all of your information, you may be able to spot trends or patterns to help rationalize the data you've collected.

When using a brainstorming activity as a method to collect information this is a good time to use 'Post-Its'. This then allows you to physically move similar ideas and comments into logical themes.

Similarities and differences

On a similar basis, another way of synthesizing the information you've collected is to look at similarities and differences. This can be a comparison between the different pieces of information themselves – in other words, in what ways are the pieces of information similar and in what ways are they different from each other?

Another useful comparison is to consider in which ways the situation being considered is similar to other situations you have experienced before and in which ways is it different?

Priorities

It can sometimes help to identify the most critical elements of information – the information which has the most impact on your final decision-making. Label information as either high, medium or low priority to ensure you primarily focus on the most important information.

Behaviors

Given that this activity is about bringing together potentially disparate pieces of information and making sense of them, one of the most important supporting behaviors is *Conceptual Thinking*. As with all behaviors, if this isn't one of your strengths you may need to consider enlisting the support of someone who is strong in this behavior.

149

Evaluating The Risks

When making decisions it's critical to consider the risks associated with choosing each of the available options as well as considering any risks associated with not making or delaying a decision.

It's all about probabilities
Risk, by nature, can only be assessed in terms of a probability and there can therefore be no certainty that the outcome will turn out as you expect. The probabilities of all the options, whether determined in a structured way or just as a 'best guestimate', will inevitably form a part of your final decision.

Past experiences
One of the best ways of determining risk is to look at similar past experiences and their outcomes. If you or others have previously faced similar situations it may be possible to examine how these eventually played out. How likely is it that your current scenario will follow a similar path to those previous examples?

Bottom up
In some circumstances it may be possible to examine statistical information to calculate probabilities from scratch. This will generally only be a viable option where you are dealing with large amounts of data relating to behaviors or attitudes and where the expense of collating and interpreting the data justifies the effort.

Best estimation
Sometimes the only option will be a very unscientific estimate based on limited facts. This approach, whilst not ideal for larger decisions with the potential for significant losses, may be appropriate when a pragmatic approach is required. Rather than leaving your evaluation to complete chance, still try to apply at least a minimal amount of logic and rigor to your estimation.

Hot tip

'Guestimating' can sometimes be the only available option but try to include as much rigor in your judgement as you can.

Mitigating Risks

There are two principal reasons for trying to understand the risks associated with a business decision:

- To determine the potential outcome of choosing a particular option or course of action and so help your decision making

- To consider any available tactics that you can employ in order to mitigate the identified risks

Prevention rather than cure

When considering the mitigation of any identified risks, the best option is to consider ways in which the risk itself can be reduced or even eliminated, in some cases through pre-emptive action.

It should be possible to brainstorm most of the possible scenarios that could result from your chosen path of action. Once you've done this you may be able to adapt the initial approach to your chosen option in order to lessen the potential negative effects.

Where it's not possible to take pre-emptive action it is still advisable to consider what actions you will take should things not go as hoped. It is far better to have thought these through prior to the risk presenting itself than to suddenly find yourself presented with a scenario with no opportunity to prepare.

Unknown unknowns

Of course, however well you prepare and explore all the possible scenarios, there is still the chance that things will go differently to your predictions – these may be positive or negative. Where appropriate, you may be able to build in contingency plans or a buffer in the form of additional time, resources or money. Even then, this may not be enough – such is the nature of risk.

Beware

Risk by its very nature is not totally predictable. Wherever possible, build in contingencies to cover the unforeseen.

Making The Decision

What you will have hopefully picked up so far from this chapter is that there is a lot you can do before making a decision by equipping yourself with relevant information. The ideas we have described for gathering data, analysis and evaluation of the risks may need to be part of a formal process involving an entire project team. For smaller issues it may merely be a simple set of thought processes taken by you as the decision maker.

The most important point is that you ensure some such process takes place so that the decision itself is not just left to a guess or, worse still, a gamble.

Instinct

You may have made some decisions based on what you could describe as a 'gut reaction' or instinct. While this may appear a risk, it may not be quite such a gamble as it initially appears.

That decision, based on a gut reaction, will most likely be based on a semi-conscious evaluation based on your years of experience and previous judgements. Your decision will most likely be based on an internal evaluation of the facts as you perceive them. So it's not necessarily all bad to trust your 'instincts'.

Decisiveness

We may be advocating that you take steps to thoroughly examine and evaluate the various options available to you, but this is not to say that the making of the final decision needs to be a slow drawn out process. Once you are satisfied you've considered all the necessary information, it's normally far better to just get on and make your decision.

Any further delay may have a negative impact on the final outcome. Furthermore, any hesitation may be seen by others as a lack of confidence – either in yourself as a leader or in your chosen option. Neither of these is helpful.

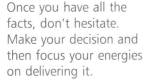

Hot tip

Once you have all the facts, don't hesitate. Make your decision and then focus your energies on delivering it.

External pressures

Rarely will decisions be made without there being some element of pressure. This pressure may be a time constraint or perhaps a fear of the competition beating you to an outcome. Probably the most difficult pressures to deal with are those from others – from your boss, your peers or from clients. They may be trying to influence your decision or just be driving you to make a decision as quickly as possible.

Beware

Don't be pressurized into making quick or rash decisions based on other's biased agendas or unrealistic time pressures.

In these situations you need to have the strength, confidence and resilience to see through your decision-making process in a rational and thorough way. Avoid being forced into making a rushed or rash decision.

Don't look back

Once you've made your decision, move on. There's rarely any benefit in continuing to replay the decision-making process. Your focus will either need to move on to other pressing issues or to implementing your decision. Once you've made your decision it is unlikely that revisiting the issue is going to be of benefit – unless you have since discovered additional information.

Supporting behaviors

The two main supporting behaviors for this final act of making the decision come from the *Self-Management* cluster. They are *Self-confidence* and *Resilience*. They may also be supported by the behavior *Focus on Achievement*.

Whose Responsibility?

The buck stops here

For most decisions responsibility lies with just one person. As a leader responsible for making decisions, you may wish to involve a number of other people to help inform you but ultimately, the responsibility for making the decision itself will normally be down to just one person – you.

Decision-making by committee

Some business decisions need to be taken by a decision-making board such as a Board of Directors. These are normally decisions being made as part of a governance process. If all normal day-to-day decisions were made in this way, the organization would be very likely to fail.

Decision making by committee is very ineffective for so many reasons:

- The time needed to fully brief everyone – to explain the underpinning issues relating to the situation; all the available options and the consequences of each would be significant

- With no one person responsible for making the decision there cannot be the same sense of accountability. Should things not go to plan – everyone will blame everyone else

- Leadership is about driving through a vision. This vision can be easily driven off course if decisions relating to that vision are left to be made by a committee

- Decisions made by committee often require consensus and therefore, when making tough decisions, a committee will tend towards the low-risk, middle position

Don't forget

Involving others in gathering information is not the same as sharing the responsibility for making the decision - the latter is not normally an effective solution.

Delegating responsibility

When delegating work to others, be very clear from the outset who has the responsibility for making decisions at each point along the way.

Having delegated a piece of work to an individual, unless you explicitly state who is responsible, there is a danger that they may go off enthusiastically making critical decisions on the false assumption that they had full responsibility for making such decisions. That's great if it was your intention but could be extremely damaging if it was not!

Conversely, you may find an individual constantly returning for you to make decisions when you had expected that they make these decisions as part of their overall delegated authority.

When things go wrong

When things go wrong don't be too quick to lay blame on the individual. It is not always about bad decision-making or judgement – remember that all decisions carry with them risks based on a series of probabilities.

That said, knowing who was responsible for making a decision can be important, especially when determining whether someone's experience and judgement can be relied upon for future decisions.

When things go right

Just as importantly, note when individuals have made good decisions and ensure they get the appropriate praise and recognition, assuming it was not just a matter of good luck.

Don't forget

Your role as leader is to recognize success. Look out for situations where individuals have made good decisions.

Learning From The Outcomes

We stated earlier that once you've made a decision you should avoid replaying the decision and instead move on. This is from the perspective of re-opening up the issue and the decision-making process given its waste of your time and emotional energy.

Having said that, there's a lot to be gained from revisiting the process you went through once you know the eventual outcome. Equating the two provides a great opportunity to learn from the experience and, in particular, to evaluate whether your analysis of the situation and your subsequent judgement was sound.

Hindsight

Even here, there is little point in beating yourself up over the decision you've made. Remember that your decision was made based on the facts available to you at that time – not, as they say, with the benefit of hindsight.

Improving your decision-making

As we'll explore in detail in the next chapter, self-analysis can be a very useful way of learning and developing as a leader. Exploring and understanding your actions and behaviors and the resultant outcomes can be very enlightening.

In the case of decision-making there is the additional benefit of helping to add to your experience as a decision maker and so refine your judgement when faced with similar issues in future. On Page 150 we highlighted how past experience can be a useful indicator when determining risk. This decision can be another to add to your database of experience.

Hot tip

Learn from each decision you make. Your experiences can make a big difference to future decisions you need to make.

Learning cycle

As with any activity you can utilize a simple learning cycle to ask yourself some reflective questions and so learn from the experience:

Remember this learning cycle. We will be coming back to it when we discuss your development in the next chapter.

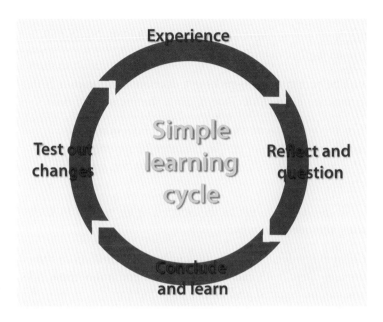

Reflective questions

Here are just a few questions to ask yourself to reflect and help focus on the learning opportunities:

? How well did I gather and sort the relevant information needed to inform my decision making?

? How well did I analyze the issues to fully understand the situation?

? Once I had all the facts, how decisive was I?

? How closely did I predict the final outcome and any of the risks that I identified?

? How would I approach this issue differently next time?

Summary

- Before making any decisions you'll need to ensure you gather all the relevant facts that will inform your eventual decision

- Remember that time can impact on the eventual outcome of a decision so don't take too long analyzing the facts

- Once you're in a position to make your decision, make it without further delay and then act on it

- Don't be pressured into making a decision against your better judgement or a rash decision against the pressure of time

- Once you've gathered all the necessary information you need to make sense of it – in Chapter 10 we provide you with some resources to find more information on possible techniques

- The simplest way to get to the bottom of an issue is to keep asking the question 'why?'

- Behind every decision there should be an evaluation of the risks associated with each option – once you know these risks some can be negated and others prepared for

- Instinct can form the basis for making decisions if, underpinning this, is a sub-conscious reliance on past experiences

- Only look back at your decision as a way of learning from the situation. In particular, determine whether your decision worked out the way you expected

- Be clear who has responsibility for making decisions

- Remember or record the way your decision turned out so that you can factor this into similar future decisions

9 Your Development

Whatever your level of experience as a leader there is always so much more to learn. Not only does self-development help you become a better leader, it also helps you to stay motivated.

Self-Development

The topics covered in this book so far have been focussed on how you, as leader, work with others to get the very best performance from those you are responsible for leading. This chapter unashamedly focusses on you and an investment in your own personal development to ensure you get the best possible performance from yourself.

It's a behavioral thing

As well as being a management process, self-development is also a critical leadership behavior – this is something we looked at in Chapter 2. Some leaders tend to have a behavioral profile that naturally values self-development such that they:

- Actively seek out opportunities for personal growth

- Treat all experiences as learning opportunities – constantly reviewing their own performance

- Have clarity over their career and life aspirations and an understanding of what they need to achieve to reach their aspirations

- Seek feedback from others in order to help appraise and improve their performance

Another development paradox

As with other behaviors we have discussed, if you're not strong in this area you may need to work hard to change or manage this aspect of your leadership profile. One difficulty with this is that developing this behavior needs you to focus on your self-development which is something that you have recognized doesn't come naturally to you.

Hot tip

If you find it difficult to find time to take your own development seriously, try scheduling it in to your daily workload as if it were a project.

Even when you've reached a point in your career where you consider yourself an experienced leader, there's always more to learn – that has to be one of the most exciting aspects of leadership.

Keeping up to date

As well as developing your leadership skills and behaviors it's important to keep up to date with your knowledge and current issues affecting the sector in which you work and possibly broader global issues. This may simply be a matter of reading relevant press and media articles or it may require more structured learning in the form of continuing professional development.

Refining your development

As you gain experience, you'll probably start to realize that attending standard leadership programmes is too unfocussed as a form of personal development. Behaviors and tailored development needs cannot easily be addressed by this type of 'classroom' style training. Whilst elements of such programmes may provide useful reminders of some leadership techniques you may find that too much of the content covers old ground.

Personal Coaching

Often the most effective way of dealing with more focussed needs is through one-to-one coaching with an experienced business coach. Your coach could be your line manager (if you have one), a trusted colleague or perhaps an external consultant coach.

A good coach will work with your goals and priorities and help you to focus your mind on the most important priorities. Take a look back at Pages 116-117 to remind yourself of the basic principles of coaching.

Beware

Using a business coach can be a great way to develop but be careful that you choose someone who is structured and challenging so that sessions don't just turn into 'fireside chats'.

Talking To Yourself

Talking to yourself - we suggest in your head rather than out loud – can be a very useful technique to help focus your mind. Examples where this may be beneficial include:

- To calm yourself and ensure you have a positive mind-set in preparation for an important event

- As a way of coaching yourself over development needs where an external coach is not available

- To 'talk' yourself through the options relating to a decision you need to make

- As a way of reviewing how you performed after an event without others being aware of what you are doing

These forms of internal dialogue are often used by those who are strong in the behavior *Self-development*.

Positive mindset

Whatever the reason for your internal dialogue, it's important that this is kept positive. This is especially important when preparing yourself for an important event. Imagine yourself where everything goes to plan and you achieve the outcomes you are looking for.

Tell yourself that you can do it. Use some of the visioning techniques we described on Page 132 to make your positive dialogue more vivid and so reinforce your positive dialogue.

Watch that negative thoughts don't creep in as these can very quickly undermine your confidence and so potentially become a self-fulfilling prophesy.

Beware

Watch that any internal dialogue remains positive because negative self-talk can be just as powerful and ultimately destructive.

Self-coaching

There is no doubt that the best option is to use someone other than yourself when you need to be coached – someone who will challenge your thinking and sometimes push you to think deeper; someone who can provide an independent viewpoint when you are, perhaps, too close to an issue to think about it dispassionately.

However, using someone else as a coach isn't always possible – you may not be currently in a position to engage a coach or it's just that your current coach isn't available for you at a critical time. So, whilst there are clearly limitations to coaching yourself, this may be the only option available to you.

It is still advisable to follow a coaching process such as the one outlined on Page 117. This will help to keep you on track and prompt you to ask yourself questions in a structured way.

Without having someone to question and test your thinking, you'll have to be tough on yourself and constantly ask yourself if your thinking is sound and whether there are other options which don't immediately come to mind.

Review your performance

Frequently use self-talk to review the way you behaved after meetings or other activities. Ask yourself questions such as:

Hot tip

If you decide to coach yourself, you'll need to remain very disciplined in your approach and we suggest you use a defined process to ensure you cover all the aspects you need to.

163

? How well did I pick up the mood of the meeting and the different non-verbal signals used by others?

? How well did my interactions and behaviors support the way the meeting went?

? How will I improve my approach next time I'm faced with a similar situation?

Development Opportunities

Almost every experience you are presented with during your working life can be treated as a development opportunity. Once you recognize this fact you can take advantage of every one of them and, in some way, grow from the experiences. Some people, regrettably, don't see these opportunities to learn and, instead, drift through their work lives without even a thought to the potential opportunities they are missing.

Learning about yourself

Every time you are faced with a situation, whether it's a meeting, the analysis of some data or even just handling emails, you will be making decisions over your approach. Become conscious of the thought processes you make, the actions you take and, if possible, which behaviors you bring into play in support of your activities. Use these experiences to help understand your behavioral profile and to question why you do things the way you do.

What impact do your values have on the decisions you make and the actions you take? What do these experiences tell you about your underlying motivational profile? Take a look back at Page 92 and ask yourself what motivations are driving you to do the things you do?

We described a simple learning cycle on Page 157. Based on this, learn from your experiences by firstly reflecting and questioning.

Seek new challenges

Don't allow yourself to settle into working within your comfort zone. Actively seek out opportunities that will stretch yourself – either intellectually, physically or emotionally.

Be hungry to take on new knowledge, skills or responsibilities. Seek to keep your mind active and stimulated by constantly looking for new challenges.

Linking to your goals

The most useful development opportunities are those that link to your career and life goals and that will help you to achieve some element of these.

Using the principles outlined in Chapter 6 relating to the development of others in your team, determine the priority areas for your own development plan that will help you achieve your overall goals. Consider what actions and experiences will help close your development gaps.

Rather than waiting on the off-chance that a development opportunity will arise, pro-actively seek out situations that will develop or test out new skills or elements of a behavior based on your development plan.

Testing yourself

Providing you're not likely to expose the organization or yourself to any undue risk, use new experiences to test yourself and particularly to try out new skills, techniques and behaviors. Don't expect things to go perfectly the very first time you try something new. It's reasonable to expect that initially you may be clumsy or awkward in your approach.

If possible, warn people that you're trying out new techniques and, where necessary, explain that they are going to be your 'guinea pigs'. If you have built up the right supporting climate within your team, they should accept this and make allowances.

Hot tip

Focus on just one or two priority development areas rather than trying to tackle too much at once. Start with a few 'quick wins' or fundamental areas first.

165

Profiling Your Personality

Many of the elements of leadership we've been exploring concern different aspects of your personality:

- Your goals

- Your motivations

- Your behavioral strengths and weaknesses

- Your values

Hot tip

It's useful to get the views of others during your deliberations, if only to sense-check your thinking and to get a second opinion.

While describing these elements we have suggested you think about your own profile in relation to each one. In Chapter 10 you will find some additional exercises and pointers to further resources to help you gain a more accurate picture of your personality.

More in depth

You should hopefully find these exercises give you some useful insights. However, you may want to explore elements of your personality in more depth – something that can be achieved through psychometric assessment or personality profiling.

Range of options

There are very many options available that can provide a more robust analysis of your personality. For example:

- Online psychometric or personality questionnaires

- Behavioral competency-based interview and feedback

- Psychometric assessment using a consultant trained to provide personalized feedback

- Feedback based on a 360 degree analysis involving your team, peers, manager and possibly other stakeholders

You may choose to combine two or more of the above in order to provide a more accurate profile of your personality.

Be honest with your responses

These same psychometric analysis tools are often used as part of a selection process by employers when recruiting. Understandably, therefore, some people feel concerned about completing such tools and will often try to adapt their responses in an attempt to alter their resultant profile. This is never a good option, especially when the assessment is being used as the foundation for your personal development process.

You should, by now, have realized that there are no right or wrong personality profiles and for the purposes of understanding your own personality it is critical that your profile and any feedback accurately reflects you. Only then can you accurately determine the most appropriate development to help you grow as a leader.

Combine the outputs

Don't just rely on a single assessment and then base all your development on this. Try to combine the outputs from a number forms of assessment. Sense-check the results from a formal psychometric assessment with your own conclusions from exercises you have completed from this book.

How do all these results compare with your own views about yourself and with what you have heard others say about you?

Take your time

Sometimes it can take a while to fully comprehend and assimilate the most important messages that result from feedback you receive. Avoid jumping to immediate conclusions but, instead, give yourself the time and space to let what you've heard sink in.

Encouraging Feedback

Encourage those that work with you – at all levels – to give you honest feedback on your performance as a leader. This openness to accept constructive criticism, whether positive or negative, can only help build a positive climate of trust and openness with those in your team.

Accepting criticism

If someone has taken the time and trouble to provide you with criticism do not become defensive over what you hear. Listen (or read) carefully and, if necessary, ask questions to clarify what is meant. Finally, thank them for their observations.

Once you're aware of criticism you will need to decide what to do about it. You may be tempted to dismiss it, convincing yourself instead that the individual has other motives in bringing the issue to your attention. Of course this may be the case but, before you do dismiss the feedback, think about what they have told you and what you can learn from it.

If what they have said is justified, it is important to take positive action to bring about the necessary changes in the way you work. If the individual (and others) see you have taken on board their feedback, they will be encouraged that they are being listened to.

Accepting praise

You may, of course, receive positive feedback or praise for the way you have performed. Accept this graciously by thanking the individual and avoid undermining the feedback by belittling its importance or passing it off as a chance occurrence.

Beware

When asking for feedback, you need to judge whether you think people are being honest with their responses or just telling you what they think you want to hear.

Using a Mentor

In Chapter 6 we described the role and benefits of a mentor from the perspective of you being the mentor. You may want to consider using a mentor to support your role as a leader. A mentor can help by:

- Being a general source of support and guidance

- Acting as a sounding-board when you need to make important decisions

- Challenging and testing your thinking relating to your vision and business direction

Choose carefully

Your choice of mentor is very important – spend time considering who would be the most appropriate person to act as your mentor.

At the level you're likely to be working at, you will need to have considerable trust in your mentor's business experience and judgement. At the same time, you will want to choose someone who can provide all of the above functions without becoming overly directive, controlling or interfering.

Look outside

You may find that the best mentor is someone completely outside of your own organization. This will ensure their perspectives on issues are relatively neutral and untainted by the same issues you are facing.

Agree ground rules

Whether you are the mentor or mentee, it's important to set ground rules at the start of the mentoring relationship covering issues such as:

- Confidentiality

- Frequency of meetings and availability of the mentor

- The scope of topics up for discussion

- Openness of any feedback

Beware

Avoid using a close friend or business colleague as a mentor as some of the issues you may need to discuss could become awkward to discuss openly.

Keeping a Development Log

When development opportunities are very explicit – say, in the form of development courses or workshops – it's relatively easy to recognize the learning that can be derived from the experience. It is not always so easy to determine or to recognize the learning in less formal learning experiences. But given how much learning occurs in these less formal situations it's important not to let these go by without recording their impact towards your overall development goal.

Keep a development log to record both the planned and unplanned learning opportunities that you experience during your working day. On the opposite page you will see an example of a development log that you can adapt to record your development activities.

Development goals

Start by stating as clearly as possible what you need to achieve as your development goals. Take a look back at Chapter 5 if you need to remind yourself how to set clear goals. Be careful to express these as goals to be achieved not as the development activities themselves.

Plan and record your activities

Where possible, plan development activities that will help you achieve your goals and also note when you expect to complete them by. Take a look at the list of possible learning activities on Pages 176-7 if you need more inspiration.

Other activities may be unplanned but could still help towards your development goals. Make sure you recognize these and record them in your development log at the time they occur.

Keep it up-to-date

It's all too easy to just put your development log away in a drawer somewhere and forget about it. You may say to yourself that you will get around to bringing it up-to-date but once the event or activity has past it's never so easy to recall what you have learnt from an experience.

Ensure you regularly review your goals and record your progress – however small – towards your development goals. Once you achieve a goal congratulate yourself before establishing your next most important development goal to focus on.

Hot tip

If you decide to maintain a development log then don't forget to record the less formal development actions such as reading or attending meetings.

Example log

Here is an example of a log completed for a development goal relating to decision-making:

Development log

Development goal

To become a more inspirational and confident presenter so that when I'm presenting to groups of 40+ I feel relaxed and can hold their attention with a well stuctured and informative talk. (Ratings of at least 7/10 on feedback)

Planned development actions	By when?	Progress notes	Date completed
Read 'Giving Great Presentations In Easy Steps'	End of April	Read through – some useful pointers	20 April
Volunteer to present at local business club	June	Went quite well but still need to work on structure	14 June
Ask mentor to observe and assess my next presentation	July		

Unplanned activities	Key learning notes	Date completed
Attended a technical seminar and used the opportunity to make notes of each presenter's style	I need to feel more relaxed about working to bullets rather than sticking to a script	16 May

Hot tip

Try to devise a series of different complementary activities in support of a particular goal rather than just rely on a single action.

171

A downloadable version of this log is available from www.ineasysteps.com and the author's website. Details of how to access this is on Page 182.

Continuing professional development

Some professions require that individuals maintain a record of their continuing professional development or CPD in order to prove that they are keeping up-to-date with their technical knowledge or skills relating to their work.

This log may look very similar to the above example. Unless there is a specific demand to do so we would encourage you to focus on the quality of the development you undertake rather than trying to merely clock up a set number of hours or points.

Summary

● Taking your personal development seriously is an important differentiating leadership behavior so ensure you devote sufficient time to your own development

● You will probably find that your development needs are best met through more focussed development activities rather than just through attending untailored training courses

● One of the best ways to focus your development is through the use of a personal coach

● It's not necessarily a sign of madness to talk to yourself if that self-talk helps you to focus your thinking towards your personal development

● Regularly review your performance at the end of meetings or after the completion of significant pieces of work. Work out how you could perform even better next time

● Many experiences you will face can be treated as self-development so raise your awareness to all the learning opportunities as they occur

● As well as looking for development opportunities, look for experiences that help you to learn more about yourself and your capabilities

● A useful way to kick-start your personal development is to complete a psychometric assessment and to receive professional feedback – this can help you highlight important behavioral areas to work on

● Be honest over the completion of any assessment process otherwise the resultant feedback will be meaningless

● Encourage others to give you feedback but make sure you take the feedback positively rather than becoming defensive

● Enlist the support of a mentor to act as a sounding board and to offer general guidance

● Keep a development log so that you effectively structure your development and also keep a record of less formal development opportunities and the resultant learning

10 Useful Resources

Having read this book, you're now hopefully encouraged to find out more about leadership. In this chapter you'll find more exercises to help understand yourself as well as sign-posts to more essential resources.

Personal Values

In Chapter 2 we described the impact of personal values on your lifestyle and, in particular, the way you make decisions as a leader. On Page 53 we suggested an exercise to help you determine the values that are most important to you. Below is a listing of single word values to help stimulate your thinking. Feel free to add other values of your own:

Don't forget

It's not just about these words. It's what these words mean to *you*. Once you've chosen your words, flesh them out into meaningful statements.

174

- Achievement
- Care for others
- Challenge
- Competition
- Contact with people
- Creativity
- Democracy
- Empowerment
- Equality
- Experience
- Fairness
- Family
- Friendship
- Health
- Honesty
- Independence
- Individuality
- Justice
- Love
- Loyalty

- Money/wealth
- Openness
- Perfectionism
- Personal growth
- Power
- Pressure
- Professionalism
- Recognition
- Respect
- Responsibility
- Risk
- Routine
- Rules
- Security
- Status
- Tradition
- Travel
- Trust
- Variety
- Work/life balance

Personality Profiling Tools

We have described the use of profiling tools on quite a number of occasions throughout this book. Here are a few websites which provide more details of personality profiling tools or psychometric assessment:

- *http://www.signalpatterns.com/personality_survey*

  This is a useful free online personality test with an interesting graphical way of representing the results. Because of its brevity, you may not wish to rely too heavily on the results without other supporting evidence.

- *http://www.myersbriggs.org*

  On Page 141 we suggested the use of a team profiling tool such as the Myers Briggs Type Indicator. This website is the official website and is therefore a reliable source of information on the MBTI.

- *http://www.teamtechnology.co.uk/mmdi/questionnaire*

  This is another free relatively short personality questionnaire that results in a simple summary based on an MBTI format.

- *http://www.41q.com/*

  One more totally free online personality questionnaire with the same warning concerning reliability.

- *http://www.shldirect.com/iPQ/index.html*

  This is an interesting test from Saville & Holdsworth, one of the leading personality profiling organizations. It is a comprehensive battery of questions, downloadable as an app to your phone. The resultant report is geared towards providing careers guidance but has some useful feedback which will be reliably researched.

Professional advice

Whilst all of the above online options can help you to understand more about your personality, there's no substitute for being professionally assessed. The robustness of most tests used by expert consultants will lead to far more reliable results. There are many complexities to the reports themselves which benefit from being explored by someone suitably qualified to provide feedback.

Hot tip

Use a range of different assessment tools and techniques and link these to your own understanding of yourself rather than just rely on one assessment.

Ideas For Development

When thinking about development activities – whether for those in your team or for you personally – try to think more laterally and creatively than just using standard training courses, programmes or workshops. On these two pages we've tried to stimulate your thinking by suggesting a wide range of different learning and development activities.

You'll see that we have divided the activities into those more suited to learning knowledge and those more suitable for developing skills. Sometimes knowledge can underpin or support the subsequent learning of a skill and therefore more than one solution needs to be considered for a development need.

Hot tip

Choose solutions that will match the learning style of the individual as this is more likely to engage the individual and result in success.

176

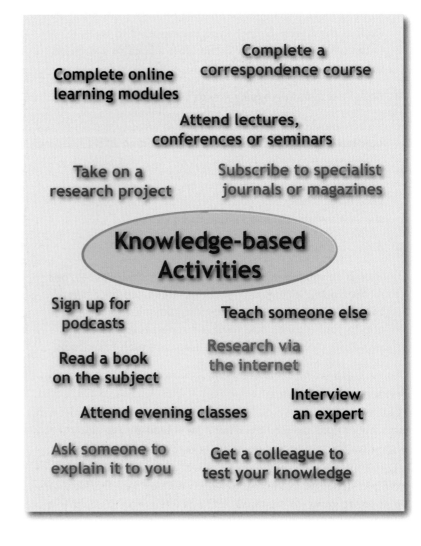

Complete online learning modules

Complete a correspondence course

Attend lectures, conferences or seminars

Take on a research project

Subscribe to specialist journals or magazines

Knowledge-based Activities

Sign up for podcasts

Teach someone else

Read a book on the subject

Research via the internet

Attend evening classes

Interview an expert

Ask someone to explain it to you

Get a colleague to test your knowledge

Work with someone else as a joint project

Attend evening classes

Take responsibility for a given task

Take on a related project

Get someone to shadow and observe you

Try copying someone else

Practise in front of a mirror

Video yourself and review your performance

Just do it!

Skills-based Activities

Practice with a camcorder

Get an expert to watch you

Role-play with colleagues

Do 'skill drills' until you get it right

Write out a process to follow

Try practicing skills on your friends

Get a colleague to test your knowledge

Shadow an expert doing it

Don't forget

These are just a small selection of possible activities to stimulate your thinking but you will probably be able to think of far more relevant specifically focussed ideas.

177

Get really focussed

All of the above options are necessarily general in nature. When you're thinking of development activities try to come up with far more focussed ideas that closely match your precise need. For example, don't just settle for 'Read a book', be specific about which book you're going to read and where you're going to get it from.

Useful Analysis Techniques

PEST or STEP Analysis

A PEST or STEP analysis is a useful way of capturing the external forces which in any way impact your organization, team or business activity. The acronym normally stands for:

- Political

- Economic

- Social

- Technical

Hot tip

These analysis tools are far better completed by a group of relevant stakeholders who represent different views on the organization and the environment in which it operates.

These four factors between them represent all of the external 'landscape'. Sometimes you will see additional factors added such as an extra 'E' for Environmental and even an 'L' for Legal although, arguably, these should fall under the original four headings of PEST.

You can try cataloguing all the factors under each of these headings on your own but for completeness it's usually far better to undertake this analysis as a brainstorming exercise, engaging a number of people each with different viewpoints and experiences.

SWOT Analysis

A SWOT analysis is another simple analysis tool. This time the acronym stands for:

- Strengths

- Weaknesses

- Opportunities

- Threats

Thoroughly listing strengths and weakness can help to create a snapshot of your team's or organization's capabilities. Linking the SWOT analysis with a PEST analysis you can use the results to determine which of the external factors within your PEST represent opportunities and which ones could represent threats.

Snapshots

Remember that both the PEST and SWOT analyses are only 'snapshots' in time and will need to be repeated from time to time to ensure they remain valid and current.

Root cause analysis

On Page 148 we described a very simple technique for getting to the root cause behind an issue or problem. There are a number of other analysis tools for establishing a root cause. Here are some more you could try together with web references to find out more about each one:

- **Cause and Effect Diagrams** – also known as fishbone diagrams because of the resultant shape produced. This is a great way of trying to understand the causes of an issue if you prefer seeing things represented diagrammatically. The following page is provided by Mind Tools who, you will see, also provide descriptions for a number of other useful analysis tools and techniques:

- *http://www.mindtools.com/pages/article/newTMC_03.htm*

Beware

Avoid jumping to obvious conclusions over root causes or, worse still, thinking about solutions until you've thoroughly analyzed the root cause.

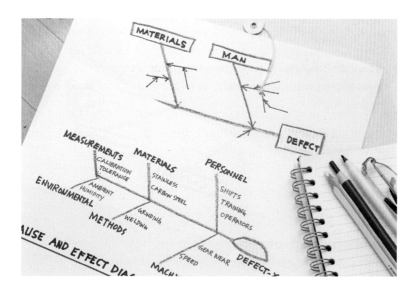

Force field analysis

Another useful analysis tool – originally developed by Kurt Lewin – is a force field analysis. This is a method for establishing the forces that support (driving) or negate (restraining) change and which, between them, balance each other. There are many sites providing details of this but, again, Mind Tools provides a good explanation:

- *http://www.mindtools.com/pages/article/newTED_06.htm*

Challenging Questions

In Chapter 9 we encouraged you to talk to yourself as part of a process of continual self-appraisal and development. Here are some critical leadership questions to ask yourself in order to continually challenge yourself and your approach to leadership. Don't just ask yourself these questions once – regularly ask and challenge yourself to remain at the very peak of your leadership capability:

Climate

- When was the last time you considered the climate of the working environment you're responsible for – what could you do to make it more positive and constructive?

- How clear are people over their roles and how their roles impact on the overall vision?

- How well do you appreciate what it is like to work under your leadership?

- How much trust do you believe others have in you and in others around them?

- How well do you encourage and consider a diversity of views and the different perspectives of others?

Your leadership profile

- How well are you utilizing your strongest behaviors?

- What support do you have in place (or need to consider) to counter your weaker behaviors?

- When was the last time you re-appraised your behavioral and motivational profile?

- Which values drive you to make decisions? – Are these values justified and relevant?

- How flexible are you at being able to adapt your behaviors to best support the work you do?

Hot tip

When it comes to issues around climate it's better to ask others how it feels with some carefully focussed questions rather than rely on your own judgement

Vision and strategy

- When was the last time you truly evaluated and challenged your strategic vision?

- How recently did you thoroughly analyze the environment in which you operate using a PEST analysis or similar?

- What differentiates your products or services to make them truly stand out from the competition?

- How well have you involved others and communicated the vision to those that are responsible for delivering it?

- Where will you and your organization be in the next five/ten years? – Be realistic based on solid evidence.

Delivering results

- How well are you utilizing the strengths and key motivations of those in your team to deliver results?

- What are you doing to ensure your vision is turned into reality and driven through to completion?

- How could you improve the accuracy and reliability of the measures you have in place?

- How clear and challenging are people's goals or objectives? – Are they SMART?

- When was the last time you celebrated success with those in your team – either individually or as a team?

Your personal growth

- How clearly defined are your personal and work-related goals? – Do you have them recorded somewhere?

- What is your current focus for your personal development?

- When was the last time you recorded a development activity in your development log?

- How frequently do you analyze your current leadership performance?

- Are you stretching yourself and giving yourself sufficient challenge or are you working within your comfort zone?

Don't forget

However inspirational your vision is, you will most likely be reliant on others to deliver it, so ensure they understand and totally support it.

181

Author's website

If you are looking for additional resources, please feel free to visit my own website. You will find, for example, printable versions of documents such as the development log described on Page 171 as well as access to many other useful resources. My website address is:

● *http://www.stepchangedevelopment.com*

Other useful resources

In addition to a number of documents provided free to download, you will also find:

● Information on the other books I have written in the series

● Details of my simple to follow business coaching process

● Access to additional leadership and coaching tips

● Access to read and comment on my blog

Most importantly, you will find a contact page on my site and (within reason!) I am happy to field any questions you have on leadership or coaching. Please also feel free to tell me about your successes as a leader – I may even include them in a future book.

Hot tip

As well as materials on leadership, you will also find other resources relating to coaching on my website.

Other Useful Websites

The problem with typing 'Leadership' into any search engine is that there is just so much material available on line that it can be very difficult to find truly useful and unbiased material. Here are some sites which do provide easy to read but helpful additional information – without also trying to overtly sell you something!

- *http://changingminds.org/disciplines/leadership/leadership.htm*

  This site provides a whole host of information on leadership, management and coaching. The above link takes you directly to the leadership section but there are many other really useful areas to explore.

- *http://www.businessballs.com*

  If you are feeling the urge to get into the detail of some of the common leadership models then this site has a wealth of background information on many aspects of leadership and management.

- *http://www.mindtools.com*

  We've already mentioned this website in relation to root cause analysis earlier but it's worth highlighting this site more generally as yet another excellent site jam-packed full of free learning material for you and for others in your team.

- *http://managementhelp.org*

  As the site itself explains - "The Library provides free, easy-to-access, online articles to develop yourself, other individuals, groups and organizations". This is a huge online library of management and leadership articles all free to read and use subject to terms.

- *http://blogs.hbr.org/ideacast/*

  This is a free weekly podcast called HBR Ideacast from the renowned Harvard Business Review. You'll find a link from this site to subscribe to their free podcasts which cover a wide range of leadership, management and business topics.

Beware

Quite a number of websites you'll visit are looking for you to buy their services. The websites listed here, on the other hand, just provide free resources.

Recommended Reading

There are so many books out there on leadership and other related topics and so your choice over which to read has, to a large extent, to be down to your personal taste over style of writing. Here are just a few suggested titles that support some of the ideas covered in this book:

- *Business Coaching in easy steps* by Jon Poole (In Easy Steps) Another of my books from the Easy Steps series that describes essential coaching skills and behaviors as well as many other related skills and techniques supporting your role as a leader. This book explains in detail the simple-to-use but extremely effective six-step coaching process

  we could only describe briefly on Page 117. See www.ineasysteps.com for title information.

  Use the process and skills described to coach others in your team or to coach yourself towards achieving your own personal development goals as we suggested in Chapter 9.

- *It's Behaviour, Stupid* by Steve Glowinkowski (eCademy Press) This excellent book centers on the role of behaviors and other aspects of personality in supporting excellence in leadership.

- *What Leaders Really Do* by John Kotter (Harvard Business School Press) A highly respected authority on the subject of leadership and change, Kotter provides a stimulating read.

- *The Empty Raincoat* by Charles Handy (Arrow) Although published in 2002, this is still a very thought-provoking (almost philosophical, on occasions) read. It provides some very challenging perspectives for any responsible leader to consider and hopefully act upon.

- *Thinkertoys* by Michael Michalko (Ten Speed Press) If you're lacking in creative inspiration then this book provides some really fun and novel ways to unlock your creative mind.

- *Goal Setting: How to Create an Action Plan and Achieve Your Goals* by Susan Wilson and Michael Dobson (Worksmart) With a title as long as this it needs little more of an introduction! This is a very practical book on goal setting.

- *The Balanced Scorecard* by Robert Kaplan and David Norton (Harvard Business School Press) Kaplan and Norton respected for popularizing the Balanced Scorecard principles – an essential tool for turning ideas into tangible outcomes.

- *Six Thinking Hats* by Edward de Bono (Penguin Books) Although first published in 1985 this is still an excellent book covering various aspects of thinking from analysis and logic through to creativity.

- *Smart Choices: A Practical Guide to Making Better Decisions* by Ralph Keeney and Howard Raiffa (Broadway Books) A very straightforward and pragmatic look at decision-making techniques covering a range of circumstances.

- *Assessment Methods in Recruitment Selections and Performance* by Robert Edenborough (Kogan Page) A good introduction into competency-based interviewing and psychometric testing should you want to conduct these yourself.

- *The Art of Possibility* by Rosamund Zander and Benjamin Zander (Harvard Business School Press) This is just a great, inspiring book that gives you the confidence to achieve the things you need to.

...And Finally

Let's go back to the theme we introduced at the very start of this book – being true to yourself. It's critical that, whatever your role as a leader and whatever your level of experience, you be yourself rather than pretend to be a different persona that is contrived from role models or from any written material you may have read.

This book has offered many leadership perspectives for you to consider, from empowerment and motivation through to decision-making and self-development. But whatever you have gleaned through reading these pages, it is essential that you develop your own personal style of delivering these in a way that works for you and your natural strengths and personality profile.

Don't let that be an excuse for not looking to make changes – but when you do make changes, do so in a way that works for you. Of course, when you first try doing things differently, you can expect to feel awkward or uncomfortable. Hopefully those around you will note a difference and this at least shows that you are doing things differently. If this is the case, keep going!

If you do use a mentor or even just rely on the support of a close friend or work colleague, ask them to feedback any differences they note.... and when these changes in your leadership style start to make a positive difference, make a point of celebrating with all who work with you.

Good luck and enjoy the role of being an inspirational leader!

Index

U

V

W

Y